Street-Smart Survival

Street-Smart Survival

A Nineties Guide to Staying Alive and Living Well

Victor Santoro

PALADIN PRESS
BOULDER, COLORADO

Also by Victor Santoro:

Be Your Own Equalizer: How to Fight the System and Win
Techniques of Harassment: How the Underdog Gets Justice

Street-Smart Survival:
A Nineties Guide to Staying Alive and Living Well
by Victor Santoro

ISBN 0-87364-641-X
Printed in the United States of America

Published by Paladin Press, a division of
Paladin Enterprises, Inc., P.O. Box 1307,
Boulder, Colorado 80306, USA.
(303) 443-7250

Direct inquires and/or orders to the above address.

TABLE OF CONTENTS

1	Introduction
5	Threats
13	The Survivalist in Fiction
17	Threat Scenarios
21	Planning for Survival
31	Food and Water
37	Shelter
39	Apartment Survival
41	Fuel
43	Transportation
45	Medical Needs
55	Privacy Protection
69	Telling Lies for Survival
73	Surveillance Smarts
77	Physical Safety
83	Weapons
103	Legal Survival
123	Social Survival
129	Electronic Survival
135	Financial Survival
139	Proactive Survival
143	Appendix A: Forged FFLs
145	Appendix B: Police Psychology
151	Appendix C: Dropping a Dime

INTRODUCTION

The 1990s will be more complex and more threatening than any previous decade. However, the old survivalist formula of "grab guns and groceries and head for the hills" won't cut it for the nineties. Those who were predicting nuclear holocaust were wrong, and they have continued to be wrong up to this date.

The problems have changed, and our ways of coping must change as well. The most serious threats to our freedom come not from offshore, but from within our borders. Crime continues to rise. Government intrusion into our lives is still increasing. Private parties, such as market research agencies, sales organizations, and private security agencies invade our privacy more than ever before. The worst news about this last threat is that it's out of control because there are no Constitutional guarantees against intrusion by private parties.

While old threats appear to be fading, others are increasing, and new ones have appeared. Cities, where most people live, are worse than ever, and certain areas are literally war zones. The possibility of nuclear annihilation is remote today, but low-grade, home-grown threats can be as deadly. Others, which don't threaten our lives, threaten our lifestyles, and while not deadly, they can be very disruptive.

High-Grade Threats

Threats from war, epidemic, or terrorism can be lethal. The terrorist threat is real, although small, but many people underrate the ripple effect. We'll examine how terrorism can affect people remote from its source.

Among the threats that do not cross national frontiers are riots and civil disorders. Street crime can also be deadly. There are also threats from people and institutions which are supposed to help you, such as police and medical personnel.

Low-Grade Threats

These are threats to life-style and can be local or widespread. A major depression is a threat to life-style, whether it affects only your own country or the world. A worldwide depression that starts elsewhere can eventually spread to your country.

Recessions, labor crises, and events which affect livelihood are also threats to life-style. Major service strikes in industries such as transportation and garbage collection are usually nuisances, although others, such as police or fire department strikes, may be remotely life-threatening.

Included in this category are commodity shortages, some of which we've already experienced, which can cause economic disruption. Oil is an obvious one, and sabotage of oil-producing facilities, including wells, refineries, ships, and storage tanks, can produce severe economic repercussions.

There are still lower-grade threats, which threaten only your life-style. Airport security, in response to what public officials perceive as terrorist threats, can affect you if you're traveling. Other examples include employee screening questionnaires, drug testing, and various invasions of privacy by private parties. You need to know how to counter or avoid these sophisticated attacks upon your privacy and how to use the invaders' own weapons against them.

Coping with Threats

In this book, we're going to look at a variety of real

threats and show how real people cope with them. We'll see that some threats are easy to avoid, requiring only the simplest precautions. Others, such as second-hand cigarette smoke, are impossible to avoid without migrating to the wilderness. We'll also see that some threats come from unexpected quarters, from the very people who you expect to help you.

Although we're going to discuss weapons, this isn't a "Rambo" book, describing a large variety of weapons and how to use them. Unfortunately, most of the threats facing you today aren't the sort that you can handle with weapons. You can't shoot a virus, strangle a power failure, or stab an economic recession. You also have to understand that there are some threats against which you won't be able to do anything.

This is a workbook more than a straight text. It contains checklists, exercises, and calculations that the urban street-smart survivalist can use to plan for survival.

Survival Strategy

Today, a good portion of being prepared is being "street-smart." Knowledge is power, and knowing what to do or not to do is just as important as the will to survive.

The most important point is that you can't protect yourself against everything. Your employment and life-style make this impossible. Your job probably depends on your being within commuting distance, and this makes it impossible to move yourself and your family to the remote areas of Montana or the Yukon. If you were financially independent and able to set up a remote retreat, you might be unable to provide education for your children or reach medical care if you needed it urgently.

Some survival precautions are so basic, and so obvious, that we'll skim over them. These include avoiding self-destructive habits, such as smoking, and taking positive steps to ensure your security. Locking your home and car doors, wearing seat belts, and so on, are all common-sense precautions that you already know.

A basic principle of survival is to avoid unnecessary fights because they dissipate your strength, but if you decide to fight, fight like hell. This applies both to individuals and to nations. A person who responds to every challenge or problem by fighting is either going to end up defeated or in jail. Likewise, we see what happens to nations that get involved in a series of wars. The United States has played "911" for many small problems around the planet during the last few decades, spending lives, money, and other valuable resources, while other countries stayed out of the conflicts and built up their industries. This has given them the competitive edge in trade and education, while the United States has depleted its economic resources and gone deeper into debt than it can afford.

This is why you have to be practical and set priorities. You have to assess the most likely threats and decide whether you can cope with them. The old cliché "discretion is the better part of valor" is especially true today.

Another part of survival strategy is to keep a low profile to protect your privacy. We'll cover this closely in the "planning" section (see Chapter 4, "Planning for Survival").

THREATS

Threats will probably endanger your life-style more than your physical safety. A power failure simultaneously affects thousands or even millions of people. Even the most hard-working mugger or terrorist can't attack more than a few people in one day. You may be killed in a traffic accident, but the odds of having your car stolen are much greater.

The Threat Ceiling

No matter how devastating a threat may be, it can only kill you once. If you're at ground zero, it doesn't matter if it's a tactical nuke or a supermegaton weapon: you're simply vaporized, and "that's all she wrote." It's also the end of the line if you're crushed by a cement truck or beaten to death by a band of muggers. This is the upper limit.

There may be one higher grade, depending upon your situation. You may value the lives and well-being of your family more than you do your own, and you may consider your death an acceptable risk to ensure your family's safety. This can motivate you to hold off a band of street thugs, at the risk of your life, to give your family time to escape.

Nuclear Threats

History now shows that nuclear threats were vastly overrated. Let's see why.

The end of the Cold War, and of the Warsaw Pact, have

greatly reduced the risk of all-out nuclear war. Despite the alarmists who predicted that a hot nuclear war was imminent, it never materialized during forty-five years of cold war.

The only two nuclear bombs ever used in war were those dropped on Japan, which was already near defeat. There was no significant Japanese nuclear program and no risk of retaliation. Once the U.S. and Soviet Russia had nuclear arsenals and delivery systems, the main effort was preventing unauthorized use by subordinates, not planning an attack. The reason is obvious.

Traditional warfare involved sending the troops out to fight and die, while the leaders remained safely behind the lines. Defeat did not necessarily result in death for the leaders, but merely surrender of conquered territory and forced disarmament. Hirohito, the Japanese emperor, remained in office long after his country's defeat, although several Japanese generals faced trial and execution for "war crimes." Hitler killed himself, and Mussolini died at the hands of his own people, yet many German, Italian, and Japanese political and military leaders survived, some to serve NATO, and others to write their memoirs. The prospects of personal survival are dimmer today.

The destructive power of nuclear bombs makes victory in the usual sense impossible after a full-scale nuclear exchange. Civilian economies, populations, and national leaders would be targets. Some war plans include a "decapitation option," a massive attack on enemy headquarters to destroy command centers. A leader certain that he, his staff, family, servants, security guards, and even pets will perish in nuclear fireballs during the first minutes of war has to be very careful. The deterrent works, and it has worked for more than forty-five years, on both sides. One important reason it's worked is that leaders on both sides have been fairly rational. Both the American and Soviet systems are fairly stable, unlike those of some Third World powers.

Certain leaders of minor powers, such as Libya's Muammar Khadafi, have developed reputations for instability.

Vulnerabilities

Which areas of the country are the most vulnerable to nuclear attack, and which are the safest? Nobody really knows. None of those who make up lists of target areas have a hot line to the Kremlin, and their choices are only speculative.

We also have to look at political vulnerability of the target, increasingly important in an era when nuclear terrorism is becoming possible. A political terrorist would be more likely to plant a nuclear bomb in New York City, which houses the United Nations, than in Albuquerque. Washington, D.C., is noted for drugs and crime and is practically worthless as a place to live, but it's the seat of the U.S. government, a prime target. To the terrorist, an annihilating strike that purges half a million people from welfare rolls is irrelevant, but one that wipes out the central government is all-important.

The best we can do is to try to anticipate likely targets, without any certainty that our hypothetical target list will be the one an enemy will follow. In this regard, it's important to note that many "survivalist" writers live in or near areas that seem to be prime targets. The major "survivalist" magazine, *American Survival Guide,* is published in the Los Angeles area.

One of the less-publicized facts about nuclear terrorism is that it isn't necessary to build a nuclear bomb to cause widespread destruction and loss of life. Using conventional explosives to pulverize and disperse low-grade radioactive material is a cheap and dirty technique, but it can be very effective. Instead of an annihilating blast, the toxic effects of radioactive isotopes will snuff out lives for years.

Exercise:

Evaluate the area in which you live. Answer the following questions:

- Are there any military bases within thirty miles?
- If so, are they training bases or strategic ones?
- What political value does your area have? Is it a state capital, financial center, or does it have a large ethnic population?
- Are there any hills or other obstructions that might shield you from the effects of an attack on them?
- How large is your city?
- Can you relocate to the other side of town or an outlying suburb for greater safety?

Biological Threats

Nuclear technology requires expensive and specialized equipment, which has given major powers some control over it. Biological weapons, on the other hand, require only a special laboratory, using commonly available equipment. A biological laboratory is clean, low-profile, and easy to hide.

Nuclear weapons testing produces large amounts of light, heat, and radioactivity. Even underground testing results in tremors detectable by sophisticated sensors. Biological weapons testing can take place indoors, making it undetectable. Burial or cremation of test animals hides the evidence. In some countries, there may even be human experimentation on condemned criminals or ethnic groups the government considers suitable for extermination. Disposal of expired human test subjects in total secrecy is practical in a closed or primitive society.

Occasionally, something goes wrong with these experiments. Gruinard Island, off the Scottish coast, will be uninhabitable for many decades because of experiments with anthrax and other germs during World War II.[1] In Utah, an aerial dispersion experiment that went wrong resulted in spraying thousands of sheep in Skull Valley with the nerve gas VX.[2] There have been rumors that AIDS is the result of an accidental release of an experimental mutated virus.

The flu epidemic of 1918-1919 might have been the result of a biological weapon. It began on the Western Front and was so contagious that it quickly spread to most European countries, and then the United States, eventually causing more than 20 million deaths.[3] About 12 million deaths occurred in India, a country far from the Western Front. Incredibly, the flu also spread to remote villages and islands. If this indeed began as a biological attack upon German forces by the Allies, it backfired severely, and it's not surprising that it's been kept top secret for decades.

An accidental release of a biological agent would be a severe threat, but there would be little you could do about it in most cases. Governments cling to secrecy, partly to avoid causing panic, and partly to avoid embarrassment and blame. Infection could hit you before you knew anything was wrong.

One very effective protective step you could take if you learned of the accident before you became infected would be to quarantine yourself from the rest of the population. This can work in the heart of the city and would protect you and your family against all but the most contagious air-borne agents. A room of the sort used for a fallout shelter would be perfect, especially if it were possible to seal it. The only problem that might come would be from other people, if they were aware that you were a survivalist and wanted some of your supplies. A hideout in a remote location would be better for avoiding exposure to a biological agent, but it would entail the disadvantages of isolated living.

Electronic Threats

Computer viruses are easier to create than biological ones. A desktop computer is enough equipment for a skilled programmer seeking to assemble a virus. This can take place even in Third World countries, and indeed, it has already happened. The "Pakistani Brain" virus was the product of the two Farooq Alvi brothers, who ran a computer business in Lahore, Pakistan.[4]

Marauders

There's been much concern over defense against marauding bands. While this may become a serious problem, it's important to keep in mind that a disaster will probably kill or injure criminals as well as good folks. Even with the much-anticipated "breakdown" of law and order, most people will probably continue to behave the way they have all their lives.

The formal structure of maintaining law and order will certainly change. Citizens' committees, in normal times labeled "vigilantes," will probably predominate. Trials will be short and swift, and penalties will probably be limited to exile or execution, as there won't be resources to maintain a long-term prison system.

In low-grade crises, we can expect martial law, with the military supplementing the police in maintaining public order. A serious problem would be the prison population. During a severe crisis, it might not be possible to continue running the prisons as before, and indiscriminately releasing convicts into the general population is unthinkable. It would be surprising if the government's secret emergency planning did not contain provisions for the emergency execution of the prison population should maintaining the inmates become impossible. The quickest method would be a general "lock-down," confining all inmates to their cells, after which a special team would insert nerve gas into the cellblocks. This would also be the most humane method, because it would spare prison guards the duty of shooting the inmates, with the delays involved. A slower but more selective method would be to screen inmates and liquidate only those convicted of violent crimes.

Plans often don't work as foreseen. Disposal of dangerous inmates might be more difficult than anticipated, and those assigned to the job might not report for work during a crisis. This is why we have to face the prospect that there might be dangerous escapees roaming the country, preying on people, without the police to inhibit them.

Terrorism

Terrorism is sensational, which is why many people, including government officials, have a distorted understanding of its effects. Twentieth century experience with terrorism has shown two basic facts: terrorism is very limited in its immediate effects, and its second-hand effects are very widespread and out of proportion to actual destruction.

Terrorism actually kills few people. In 1980, for example, about 1,800 people were murdered in ordinary street crimes in New York City. This was the same as the total number of fatalities in the Northern Ireland war, which by then had been running for more than ten years. An average of twenty-five Americans die each year in terrorist incidents on foreign soil, a small number compared to the numbers murdered in even a medium-size American city. Fewer than a dozen people have died from food and drug tamperings, as in the Tylenol incident, although in 1988 about 6,300 people died of accidental poisonings caused by solids, liquids, and gas, according to National Safety Council figures.

Second-hand effects are both far-reaching and profound. Drug manufacturers have spent millions of dollars developing tamper-resistant packaging as a result of the Tylenol poisonings. As a result of aircraft hijacking, which killed very few people, airlines and airports have procured metal detectors and hired many additional security personnel, increasing the costs and delays for passengers. Even the threat of terrorism can impose delays and disruptions at airports. When Saddam Hussein appealed to Arabs everywhere to support him, security at the world's major airports went up several degrees, even though Saddam had never specifically threatened attacks against airlines. Airlines stopped accepting curbside luggage check-in, and only passengers with tickets were allowed onto the concourses. There was more intensive searching of passengers, including physical frisks and cross-checking of checked baggage with bags actually boarding. Airline personnel were told to report any unattended luggage because a valise left behind might contain a bomb. There were several incidents of forgotten suitcases examined by bomb squad officers.

Real threats cover a wide range. Not surprisingly, imaginary threats devised by fiction writers cover as broad a field. Let's give them a once-over next.

ENDNOTES

1. Robert Harris and Jeremy Paxman, *A Higher Form of Killing* (New York: Hill and Wang, 1982), 74-80.
2. Ibid., 238.
3. Geoffrey M. Marks and William K. Beatty, *Epidemics* (New York: Scribner's, 1976), 271-277.
4. John McAfee and Colin Haynes, *Computer Viruses, Worms, Data Diddlers, Killer Programs, and Other Threats to Your System* (New York: Saint Martin's Press, 1989), 30.

THE SURVIVALIST IN FICTION

During recent years, we've seen books, motion pictures, and TV productions dealing with survival, the aftermath of nuclear war, enemy invasion, and the like. The movie *Red Dawn* was one effort in projecting an enemy invasion and occupation of this country. While the acting, characterization, and special effects were superb, the plot was thin because it was totally unrealistic. While a flash raid by a small force of paratroopers flown in under radar cover is always possible, the task of supplying and reinforcing them once they have landed is impossible. An enemy won't assign a group of his scarce and valuable airborne forces to capture an American high school in the Colorado Rockies, as happened in the film. There are too many high-priority military targets worth neutralizing to allow squandering paratroopers on marginal targets.

A series of "survivalist" novels also appeared. The hero was a medical doctor employed by the CIA, who was also a martial artist and expert shot. His income must have been considerable, even for a doctor, because he was able to make extensive and costly preparations. He had built an elaborate underground survival retreat in the American Southeast. This shelter had a hidden entrance and contained sleeping quarters, a stockpile of food and water, an elaborate arsenal, and other survival gear. After a nuclear attack, the Soviets occupied the United States, and the doctor spent several volumes coping with lawless elements and other threats while trying to find his family. Most of us don't have that combination of skills nor the luck that kept the doctor from being killed by barrages of enemy bullets.

The only traditional survivalist novel that became a classic was Oliver Lange's *Vandenberg*, recently reissued with the title *Defiance*. Gene Vandenberg, the central character, is a maverick artist who rebels against the Soviet occupation forces after the defeat of the United States. He spends some time in a Soviet brainwashing camp, gains his release, and subsequently organizes a raid against that camp. His scratch force of civilians blows up a Russian garrison, steals an armored car, and overcomes the guard force at the camp. A Russian air strike annihilates his group during the escape.

A more realistic piece of fiction for the nineties was written two decades ago and made into a successful movie starring Charles Bronson. *Death Wish* presents a realistic picture of violent crime in the big city. It also fairly presents the risks faced by anyone who tries to cope with crime on his own. The scenario takes place in New York City, which at the time had deteriorated to the point many American cities face today.

The hero, after street criminals kill his wife and rape his daughter, undertakes to purge some lawless elements. During a business trip to Arizona, he acquires a revolver and ammunition. Upon his return, he makes a decoy of himself, taking walks in lonely places, such as parks, and riding the subway late at night. Not surprisingly, he encounters muggers, whom he shoots as soon as they begin their attacks. The hero is not a superhero, and assailants injure him twice. Not being an experienced gunman, he also makes a few tactical errors, and these lead to his being injured by hoodlums and his eventual discovery by police.

The book, although fiction, serves as a practical training manual for anyone living in the big city. The film, available on videotape, is a good training tape for anyone anticipating trouble on the streets or subway. The situations and tactics depicted are fairly realistic and are good starting points for the "what-if" planning process.

Reality sometimes follows art, and one example was the result of *The Turner Diaries*, a book written by Andrew McDonald more than a decade ago, which used a plot of a right-wing organization struggling against the "Zionist" government in Washington. The core of the underground organization was "The Order," which carried out raids and assassinations against the central government and its agents. The cliche "life imitates art" may be true in this case. A real-life "Order" sprang up soon after the book appeared, perhaps not totally by coincidence, and its members armed themselves and carried out several robberies to obtain funds for their organization. They also killed Alan Berg, a successful Jewish talk-show host in Denver who made a point of baiting right-wing people and organizations on the air. The Order had a hit list, and allegedly in second place was the name of Morris Dees, a lawyer in Montgomery, Alabama, who specializes in pursuing lawsuits against the Ku Klux Klan and other similar organizations.

Survivalist fiction, although often imaginative, isn't always a good guide to reality. The better books and movies can portend the future, but the worst are destructive fantasies. Let's now look at some survival scenarios for the nineties.

THREAT SCENARIOS

Many people, especially survivalists, have tried to predict the future, but most have failed. We've heard recurrent predictions of nuclear war during the last forty years, but they've all been wrong. There have been other events, such as the petroleum crisis, which few foresaw.

It's hard to predict the future when we don't even understand the past. Historians and others are still arguing about the causes of World War II and whether the United States should have played a different role in it.

There are many scenarios for the future. Let's rank them according to a scale of credibility, so that we know how seriously to take them. There are three categories, in order of decreasing credibility:

1) Predictions of events that have already happened and probably will happen again, and which we understand. These include recessions, epidemics, earthquakes, inflation, wars, and fuel shortages. These are the most credible, and we have experience in coping with them.

2) Scenarios of events which are possible technically, given our present situation, but are less likely because they've never happened before and there is a strong reluctance to initiate them. This category includes a major nuclear war and other doomsday scenarios.

3) Events which are possible based on future developments, however improbable, placing them in a special

category of "anything is possible, if you can't prove it's impossible." These include a world government imposing a total dictatorship, a collision between planets, and other possibilities depending only on imagination.

Don't be surprised at the range of threats you face in the city. A city is a central exchange for people who prey on other people. Criminals practice economy of scale, finding many potential targets within reach. An example is the "commuter burglar," traveling to his target area each day and returning home with his loot in the evening.

Threats come not only from criminals, but from some of the mechanisms of law and order, the legal establishment, or others who you'd think are there to help you. Let's look at a few possibilities to understand the nature of the problems you face.

- You shoot someone forcing his way in through a window and call the police. When they arrive, they don't treat you like either a victim or hero, but promptly arrest you for having an unregistered firearm. More criminal charges follow.
- A telephone call tells you that your daughter has been hit by a car and is getting emergency care at a hospital. You and your wife immediately leave for the hospital, but when you arrive you find that your daughter isn't there, and nobody knows who called you. When you return home you find that it's been burglarized, and you suspect that the call was just to get you out of your home.
- A gang of youths surrounds you on the subway, threatening you and asking you for money. When they display knives, you're forced to use your legal concealed weapon in self-defense. After the police take their report and reassure you that you were within

your legal rights, you get hit with a lawsuit filed by the family of one of your attackers, alleging that you violated his civil rights.

- An armed robber shoots the store manager while you're shopping and flees. You pick up the pistol the manager has dropped and start in pursuit. A police officer responding to the robbery call mistakes you for the suspect and opens fire on you.
- One night a known shoplifter and bad-check passer enters the store you manage and begins acting suspiciously. You and another employee follow him around the aisles and decide to ask him to leave because he appears only to be seeking an opportunity to steal something. As you're escorting him outside, he becomes abusive, and when he reaches his car, he tells you that he's got a gun and threatens to shoot you. Alarmed, you and the other employee jump on him and wrestle him to the ground, where he bites your wrist. In the struggle, the suspect's windpipe gets crushed, and he dies on the scene. What would be a normal case of self-defense turns into a case of murder because the suspect turns out to be unarmed. It's a no-win situation for you, because he's a minority group member, and you're accused of "racism."
- Your wife enters the hospital for an operation that appears unlikely to endanger her life. In the operating room, she gets several units of the wrong blood type because of a technician's error, and she dies.
- A power outage in your area leaves homes without electricity and closes businesses, including your workplace. You can't afford to miss work for even a few days, and food supplies dwindle as your neighbors clean out store shelves.
- Your company begins a random drug testing program,

and one morning you're asked to urinate into a small bottle. Your test result comes back positive, even though you do not use drugs, and your career at that company is over. Finding another job also becomes very difficult.

- Your employer has suffered employee theft and hires a firm of private investigators to check out the prospects. One day, one of the investigators takes you into a small room and begins questioning you as if you're a suspect. You know that you're innocent, but you also know that if you refuse to cooperate, your employment will be in jeopardy.

None of the above scenarios are fantasies. They're all real, borrowed from actual news accounts, and each has happened to real people, perhaps even to someone you know. The wide range of threats suggests that your planning must be more comprehensive than ever before.

PLANNING FOR SURVIVAL

Much survival thinking is utopian, directed towards an ideal situation in which the survivalist has ample money, land, and other resources with which to prepare. The hard reality is that most people live in cities, which the "experts" say are the worst environments for survival. People are pinned to their locales by the need to earn a living, as jobs are sparse in rural areas and small towns.

Surviving in the urban environment during the 1990s will be different from before, because you'll have to seek other ways to prepare. You'll have to compromise with reality, because the ideal solution is out of your reach. You will probably have to prepare on a "Joe Six-Pack" budget. Many plans and preparations are not open to you, because you must not only earn a living while waiting for THE DAY, but you must live on modest means, devoting only a fraction of your income to survival.

Fortunately, there are some factors in your favor. Time, first of all, is on your side. Despite the predictions of doomsayers, a nuclear or less spectacular catastrophe is not necessarily around the corner. You don't have to do it all in one day, but it's wise not to wait until the last moment. The Persian Gulf crisis provided one example. Within days of the outbreak of hostilities, the run on gas masks had almost exhausted civilian supplies in the United States, although Iraq had no ballistic missile able to reach the United States. Still, surplus gas masks that had sold for seven dollars were now bringing fifty, and CNN carried a feature on an

American family that had set up a sealed room stocked with supplies, just in case.

Another important fact is that many preparations are useful against a variety of threats. Food, for example, is necessary whether the threat is critical or subcritical. You can make long-range plans, preparing in stages, without the need for a crash program and confident that every stage you complete brings you closer to your goal.

Flee or Stay?

This is a basic decision, but times have changed, and yesterday's advice is stale and impractical today. Urban traffic jams will get worse during the nineties. Evacuation may even be impeded by authorities, and planning to stay in place is more realistic.

One plan that needs a quick look is the "Crisis Relocation Plan" set up by the Federal Emergency Management Administration, FEMA for short. The basic principle is to move people from cities to nearby rural areas, using evacuation routes, reception areas, and supplies prepared in advance. The only point on which most people agree is a lack of confidence in it, because it's not a realistic plan. The main problems with it are arranging efficient transportation and the unwillingness of rural residents to take in evacuees. Some have suggested that residents of small towns would block roads and turn back evacuees by force.

Survival Groups

Should you plan to form or join a group, or try to survive on your own with your family?

The consensus is that the survival group has a better prospect than the individual. A group not only has more strength for defense, but it has a collection of skills to meet various threats.

Group dynamics are important. People who band together have mutual emotional support, very important in a situation likely to induce fear and degrade morale.

One basic principle in forming a survival group is that quality is far more important than quantity. A small group is better, for several reasons:

1) "Lean and mean" is more realistic than the "big battalion." A survival group cannot afford any dead wood.
2) The larger the group, the more severe are the logistics problems. Food, shelter, and transportation for a large group are always more complex than for a small one, and supplies will be scarce.
3) Security is always better with a small group. There are fewer possible leaks, and a small group is less noticeable than a large horde, in all situations.

Unfortunately, a group can't protect against many real-life threats. In some cases, authorities might even view it as a criminal conspiracy, especially if there's group stockpiling of weapons and other supplies. This is when keeping a very low profile helps.

Exercise:

- How many reliable close friends do you have?
- Do they know you're a survivalist?
- How do they feel about it?
- What skills do they have?
- What additional skills do you need, and how do you plan to acquire them? (paramedic, etc.)
- Should you approach your friends one by one, or call a meeting?
- What about weaker members of the group, such as children, the aged, and the infirm? Whom do you take along, and would you consider abandoning any of them? Better decide these matters now, instead of leaving them for later.

Keeping a Low Profile

The most important aspect of urban survival is not making yourself conspicuous. Remaining inconspicuous is called "keeping a low profile," and it's vital to your defense.

There are several important reasons for the low profile:

1) You may not want your neighbors to know that you keep a stockpile of food, ammunition, silver coins, etc. If your neighbors are like most Americans, they won't have prepared for survival, and may expect you to share your resources with them. They may even try to take your supplies by force.

2) People gossip, and news of your preparations may reach unfriendly ears. You may be burglarized one day while you're away, because guns, silver, and other supplies are valuable in normal times.

3) Certain items may be illegal or subject to confiscation. If you keep a firearm in an area where they're banned or must be licensed, an informer may tell the police. Although stockpiling food isn't illegal, during a war or other crisis the government will call it "hoarding" and may confiscate food stockpiles from prudent preparers to feed those who are unprepared.

4) Keeping a low profile also covers what you say, and keeping your mouth shut can save you legal complications. If you're foolish enough to announce to anyone who will listen that you intend to "blow away" anyone who tries to burglarize you, your words may return to haunt you. Your statement may serve as evidence of premeditation if you're prosecuted for defending yourself with a firearm. We'll look at this more closely in the "legal" section.

5) As we've seen, some political fringe organizations have attracted attention from the police and FBI. Above all,

you don't want to be identified with any of these, especially if you're not a member. If your name ever gets on one of the government's computerized suspect lists, you may find yourself a target for investigation. In a crisis, your name may even be on a "round-up" list of suspects slated for internment. This happened to enemy aliens and to Americans of Japanese ancestry during World War II, and it's reasonable to expect action against "suspects" in another crisis. Indeed, at the start of the Persian Gulf War, FBI agents were investigating Americans of Arabic ancestry.

6) Publicity and notoriety can be harmful to your financial health as well. The Internal Revenue Service (IRS) watches the news for helpful hints to tax evaders. Let's say that there's an announcement in the local paper that you've just bought a company, or that your plant has expanded its operations. IRS agents may correlate that bit of news with your tax return, wondering where you obtained the money to pay for it. If you get burglarized and the media state the value of the goods or money stolen, the IRS will be looking for unreported income by trying to trace the money that paid for your expensive jewelry or electronic equipment.[1]

7) Keeping a low profile also takes in your appearance. In Los Angeles, some street gang members have confessed that they choose victims to rob by looking for men wearing Rolex watches, because they know that a Rolex signifies big money.

A vital part of keeping a low profile is avoiding giving out information to people you don't know, especially when you don't have to. This especially includes avoiding "surveys" of various sorts that market research companies conduct. Some are telephone surveys, while others are questionnaires you get in the mail. If you think about it, you'll see the absurdity of divulging personal information to a stranger who telephones you, or of providing personal information in writing to a company that will use it for unknown purposes.

Some of the questions are very probing. You may find yourself being asked how much money you earn, for example, or how much you spend in various categories, such as cars or vacations. This information can serve to target you as a potential customer, and you may find your mailbox stuffed with more junk mail as a result. Remember also that this is different from filling out employment and insurance applications, which often contain a perfunctory promise of confidentiality. Any information you provide is not, *repeat not*, confidential, and the marketing company can sell it to anyone it wishes, including private investigators, attorneys, and the Internal Revenue Service. If your income, as declared on Form 1040, is $25,000, but you list it as double that on a questionnaire, you can be sure this will arouse a revenue agent's curiosity. Likewise, it would be surprising if the U.S. Marshal's Office fugitive apprehension program did not tap into these surveys to see which names turn up.

Some market research companies use enticements, such as the promise of manufacturer's discount coupons, to get you to divulge personal information. Another come-on is the promise that you may qualify to participate in a market survey and be paid twenty dollars an hour for your services. The phrasing is always cleverly worded to provide an escape from the promise, and once you return the questionnaire, don't be surprised if you never hear from them again.

Another way companies collect information is by having customers fill out long and detailed questionnaires to register their products for "warranties" that are mostly worthless. These questionnaires ask about your age, income, family size, home ownership, and shopping habits. When you reveal information about yourself in any of these questionnaires, you can be sure it will end up in a data bank somewhere, for access to anyone willing to pay the fee. Purchasers are usually marketing companies seeking a particular type of client profile, such as single male professionals who like to take overseas vacations.

When you see a warranty registration form packed with a product you buy, remember that the warranty is not contingent upon your answering all of the questions, unless it so states explicitly in the warranty. Don't be bluffed into providing personal information to "help" the company honor the warranty.

Yet another way private businesses obtain detailed information about you is through the questionnaires you fill out when you apply for insurance. Insurance companies depend not only on the applicant's reporting but on information that investigators can uncover. This can include your driving record, occupation, marital status, or "participation in hazardous hobbies." There may also be information about your life-style, economic status, reputation, drug or alcohol use, property location and use, and prior insurance losses.[2]

Who gets this information? One company that states it takes "great care" to protect clients' confidentiality also lists who has access:

- The insurance agent or broker
- Anyone performing a special function, such as an appraiser
- Insurance intelligence support groups
- Insurance research organizations
- A court
- A government agency
- An investigative agency
- Other insurance companies

This makes it clear that many people, including private

parties, corporations, and government agencies, have free access to any information you divulge when you apply for insurance. This is true whether you are accepted or not. It's dangerous to assume that, if they turn you down, they destroy your application. Once you're in the system, they hold onto the information. Even if they return the application to you, the information is in a computer somewhere.

Other private data banks maintain special types of information, such as people who have filed a malpractice suit against a doctor. Dockets Search, Inc., makes this information available to doctors and hospitals, and some use it to "blackball" patients who have sued doctors. The result is that, even if the doctor was incompetent, the name of the plaintiff goes into the data bank, and he may find himself the victim of discrimination. As we'll see, patients cannot find out if their doctors have ever been disciplined or sued. The same blackballing principle applies to the employee who files a workmen's compensation claim. Some employers feel that anyone who has filed a claim is an unsafe employee, and they can check job applicants out against the data bank.[3]

There are other ways to get into private data banks. If you subscribe to a gun or survival magazine, you can be sure that you'll end up on a magnetic tape or disc in a law enforcement agency computer. If you subscribe to a porno magazine, the magazine may sell its mailing list, and postal inspectors will target you for sting operations, such as "Operation Looking Glass," which we'll examine later. If your choice is a homosexual magazine, you'll be on a list somewhere as an AIDS risk, and this can stop you cold when you apply for health insurance.

Even if the publication doesn't sell its mailing list, postal inspectors can obtain your name anyway. Bulk mail is conspicuous, and postal inspectors can copy from the address labels when the magazine mails its issues.

You can also wind up in a police data bank, even without having been arrested. Police agencies normally keep files on any persons with whom they have any contact, including traffic offenders, and even witnesses to a crime. In one case, the Phoenix Police Department kept a list of possible AIDS carriers, available by computer link to its officers and to the Maricopa County, Arizona, sheriff's office. One individual found his name in the computer because he had been present during a picnic in a city park. Police noticed that several conspicuous homosexuals attended, and they entered the license numbers of all vehicles at the scene into their computer.

General survival planning is the first step. Now let's look at a few specifics.

ENDNOTES

1. Santo M. Presti, *IRS in Action* (Sherwood Communications, 1986), 39-40.
2. Ohio Casualty Insurance Company Privacy Statement.
3. *Consumer Reports* (May 1991): 356.

FOOD AND WATER

Providing for your basic needs in the city can be very difficult, because you depend on a complex supply system to deliver food and other necessities. Living off the land becomes impossible when cement and asphalt cover the earth.

Stockpiling

You should maintain a basic food stockpile for at least two reasons. First is that the food supply may be interrupted. You should also maintain a hedge against economic distress. We've had one major depression and many recessions in our century, enough to convince the most optimistic person that this threat is real.

The standard joke is that if your neighbor loses his job, it's a recession, but that if you become unemployed, it's a depression. Even without nationwide economic upheavals, the last years of the twentieth century have seen mergers, buyouts, and corporate "downsizing," all bad news to the wage earner.

Most cities have only a few days' supply of food stored. This makes the problem crucial, as a crisis would quickly empty supermarket shelves. Individual preparations can make the difference between surviving and starving.

When planning your stockpile, remember that experience has shown that you should stick as closely as possible to foods you're accustomed to eating. A sudden switch to unfamiliar foods, such as vitamin-fortified chocolate or cereal bars, can make you ill. You should taste-test all foods you're considering for your stockpile.

In calculating your food supply, you have to consider several problems. One is storage, especially if you live in an apartment. This is a major problem, although modern construction includes many more closets than older buildings.

Another problem is shelf life. Canned and dehydrated foods last for several years. Frozen foods have somewhat shorter shelf lives, but they also require an uninterrupted electrical supply, which you can't take for granted.

Also important is cost. This will probably be the deciding factor for most of us, as preparing for survival requires setting priorities. Closely related to the cost of the food is the cost of other items you need to preserve or prepare the food items. This makes frozen food a very bad choice because of the cost of the freezer and electricity. Add the cost of repairs, because any mechanical item can break down. Also calculate the risk of spoilage in case of mechanical failure or a power outage.

The only accessories you need with canned and dehydrated foods are a can opener, a cooking pot, and eating utensils. Dehydrated foods require water to prepare, and you can't be sure of getting water from the tap during a survival crisis. You can eat most canned foods straight from the can.

Make price comparisons. Check out comparable items in supermarkets and backpacker stores. You'll find that dehydrated foods labeled "backpacker" or "survival" are at least three times the price of similar items sold in supermarkets. Compare the price of a quart size of powdered soft drink mix containing sugar, such as Kool-Aid, with a similar product sold in a backpacking store.

There are certain items that are not exactly comparable. You can find freeze-dried steaks with no exact counterpart in canned goods. Freeze-dried steaks cost at least twelve dollars per pound. If you can tolerate canned roast beef in gravy, a twelve-ounce can costs less than two dollars in most supermarkets.

Convenience is also important. A freezer takes up space that you may need for other items in a cramped apartment. If you have to leave suddenly, you can always throw a few cans of food or envelopes of freeze-dried food into a box or knapsack and get out with only a few minutes' notice. Anything you take from your freezer will be very perishable, and you'll have to plan to eat it as soon as it thaws. A plastic ice chest extends its life for only a day at most, unless you can keep it filled with fresh ice. You'll also need to cook the food, and a hibachi may not be conveniently available.

If your contingency plan is to bug out, and you decide to take freeze-dried foods with you, remember that you'll also have to carry your own water or plan to find drinking water where you're going, as well as along the way. Many freeze-dried foods also require hot water to reconstitute them, and you'll have to plan for this.

If you plan to remain home, whatever happens, you won't have to spend money on expensive "backpacking" freeze-dried foods. Not having to carry food is an advantage. Stockpile vitamins as well, because you're not going to be able to eat fully balanced meals under survival conditions.

Food for Travel

Unless you plan to do your traveling in a motor home or travel trailer, you'll have to plan your food supply extremely carefully. Your planning will have to include convenience, compactness, and cooking.

Convenience requires food that you don't have to cook or prepare. This include fruits and some vegetables, as well as candy bars and jerky that you can eat on the run. This might be crucial if you have to cover ground quickly and don't have time to stop to eat.

Compactness is obvious. You need food that's not excessively bulky. This eliminates a number of otherwise suitable and tasty foods, such as potato chips.

Cooking may not be possible, but if it is, you'll need food

that's easy to prepare. No matter how much you enjoy frozen pizzas, you may not have an oven to prepare them. The most likely cooking method you'll have is a wood or oil stove, or an open fire.

A good choice is the array of military MREs, if you can obtain them at a reasonable price. These Meals, Ready to Eat, are both tasty and balanced, as well as compact. Some dislike them, however, calling them "Meals Rejected by Ethiopians." You'll have to decide that for yourself.

Exercise 1:

- How much money do you have available to buy extra storable food each week?
- How long would it take you to build up a year's supply?
- Where would you store it?

Exercise 2:

- Make up a list of food items you feel you'll need. Compare the prices for similar items from your supermarket and from a survival store. How much money can you save? Can you substitute any items?
- Can you buy any canned or dried foods on sale?

Exercise 3:

- Compile a week's emergency menu based only on stored foods. Is it nutritionally balanced? Is it tasty?

Water

Another problem is water. Right now, you take the water supply for granted because you don't have to do without it. It's available just by turning a tap. Sabotage of a pumping station by terrorists can leave you literally high and dry.

Exercise 1:

- Calculate how much water you can store in your

home, *right now*, with what you have. Include the hot water heater, waterbed, bathtub, and sinks.

Exercise 2:

- How much spare room do you have? If you don't live on the ground floor, will your floors hold the weight of a large amount of water?

Exercise 3:

- Calculate the costs of buying extra containers for water storage and the costs of different methods of water purification:
    - Which will cost the least?
    - Which is best for your situation?
    - Which takes the least weight and space?

Exercise 4:

- List ways of saving money on your survival preparations and calculate how much you can save by practicing economy.
- Can you save gallon milk jugs to hold water?
- Do you have any special containers, or can you obtain any where you work that may be useful for storing water?

SHELTER

Shelter includes any dwelling which the dweller can prepare for survival. The city dweller must make do with what he has, but even then can prepare for a wide range of eventualities. The idea of a survival "retreat" in a remote place is appealing, but not as practical as it seems. It's nice to contemplate a cabin or cave miles from nowhere, but setting one up for occupancy isn't as easy as it appears.

First, a remote refuge must be self-sufficient. Far from civilization and sources of supplies, you'll have to carry in everything you'll need, except perhaps water if there's a nearby stream or well.

Will you live there 24 hours a day, 365 days a year, or will you have to live close to your job in the city most of the time? If you have to leave your survival site unattended, you run the risk of vandalism. You also have the problem of reaching it in a crisis.

Security is another problem. In rural areas, strangers are uncommon, and you may sense a latent hostility towards any outsiders and find people you meet curious about you. Local residents may not hit you with a barrage of questions, but they'll certainly observe you making trips to your site, and inevitably someone will wander up the road to see what you've been doing. Your business will become everybody's business. That's the way it is in small communities.

APARTMENT SURVIVAL

Apartment dwellers have a special problem. They only control a small part of the building in which they live, and they have limited storage space. Practically all apartments lack the copious storage space of a private house.

Apartment Living

Choosing the apartment is the first step. When you look at your present living quarters with the perspective of a survivalist, you may be surprised to find how insecure your premises are.

A ground floor apartment offers a tremendous advantage in storage capacity, because the floor is strong. However, you have the disadvantage of easy access from street level. This can be a serious problem in high-crime areas, but street-level occupancy offers you an alternate escape route in case of fire or an assault against your front door.

Upstairs, you're more secure against assault. The higher the better. However, consider buildings next to yours. If a similar building is only across an air shaft, your security is very limited. Windows overlooking yours allow an attacker to shoot into your premises.

First, reinforce the floor with two-inch-thick planks across the entire floor area of at least one room, preferably an interior room that visitors don't get to see. This provides strength, and can make a tremendous difference if you can distribute the weight of water jugs across an entire floor. If you're concerned about flying bullets, keep in mind that wood planks stop only handgun bullets at best, and that if you really want protection you'll have to include a layer of half-inch steel.

FUEL

It makes sense to stockpile fuel while it's inexpensive and easily available. It's also smart to locate other sources, in case your primary supply becomes exhausted. If you're simply after heating or cooking fuel, almost anything will do. You can improvise a stove from any sort of large metal container and burn almost anything in it. Tree branches, old magazines and newspapers, and scrap lumber are all very practical fuels, as you can see if you watch "street people" on a cold night.

If you have storage room, collect old newspapers and magazines. Some survivalists stockpile hexamine tablets, available in surplus stores. Their main value for the armed services is smokeless flame, to avoid giving away a concealed position, but they're not as cost-effective as heating or cooking fuel.

TRANSPORTATION

This will be less of a problem in the city than in rural areas because of the short distances involved. Walking is useful for crisis reconnaissance. Motor vehicles are out because of the difficulty of storing fuel for them. Survival on a budget rules out some technically possible but exotic and expensive choices such as solar-cell cars.

The bicycle is an excellent choice, for several reasons:

- It uses no fuel
- It's cheap
- It's easy to run and maintain
- It's easy to carry over obstacles such as rubble

It can, with simple adaptation, carry a load of between three hundred and five hundred pounds. During the Vietnam War, Vietcong supply troops tied poles to bicycle handlebars and balanced heavy loads on them, walking their bikes on jungle paths. This silent and fuel-free method of transportation worked well for them.

Exercise 1:

- Do you own a bicycle?
- How much would it cost to get the materials for carrying heavy loads, and where would you store them until needed?

MEDICAL NEEDS

Survival medicine is rarely life-saving surgery performed under primitive conditions because medical help is days away or totally unavailable. Today, it more often comes down to two needs: avoiding the risks involved in conventional medical care and keeping a severely injured person alive long enough to obtain qualified medical care.

Avoiding Medical Risks

There's more to providing for your medical needs than stockpiling prescription drugs and other supplies for a getaway kit. Realistically, some of the threats come from people who are supposed to help you. Doctors play down the risks and cover up their mistakes, but your survival requires that you understand the problems, so that you can avoid the avoidable risks.

American doctors tend to be mercenary and greedy. This is why doctors' incomes rose 7.7 percent in 1989, while the annual rate of inflation was only 4.6 percent, as measured by the Consumer Price Index. In 1986, doctors' incomes rose by 6.5 percent, while inflation was only 1.1 percent, according to the 20 November 1987 issue of *American Medical News.*

What accounts for these increases? No other country has such a high rate of unnecessary surgery, for example. Doctors tend to prescribe drugs and other treatments according to the patient's financial status instead of real needs. Drugs have side effects, and some of these are serious, even life-threatening.

One government study showed that doctors with laboratories in their offices tend to prescribe tests and X rays for their patients more often than those without.[1] The average number of tests per patient was 6.23 by doctor-owned labs, while independent labs performed only 3.76 tests per patient. The average fee charged by the in-house lab was $44.82, while the independent lab charged an average of $25.48 per test.

The profit motive is not hard to understand, and it overrules considerations such as patient safety. X rays, especially those performed by dentists, are one form of abuse. Today, X rays are very safe, because high-sensitivity X-ray films need very little radiation for satisfactory exposures. While a single X ray is safe, the radiation from many is still dangerous.

Most Americans have heard the advice to seek a second opinion before undergoing surgery or expensive therapy, but not all understand the real reasons why. Apart from the profit motive, which impels some doctors to prescribe surgery more often than is really necessary, there's the problem of operative risk. Any surgery has a death rate and a complication rate. There is no absolutely risk-free surgery, and any doctor who says so is a liar. Common operative risks are anesthesia death, infection, and hemorrhage. There are between thirteen thousand and fifteen thousand deaths due to anesthesia in the United States each year. Postoperative infections are so common that nobody even collects statistics on them. Hemorrhage and postoperative bleeding are also part of the risk and are routine.

There are also less common risks resulting from human errors. One is mismatching blood types for transfusion, which can easily be fatal for the receiver. Another is administering the wrong drug in the hospital. Harried and overworked nurses do mix up patients' pills. Some nurses dose themselves with stimulants and tranquilizers because they're easily available, and this can also lead to their making errors. When they do, the results can be disastrous.

Another hazard is transmission of disease. Your doctor

does not have to be a homosexual or drug addict to catch hepatitis or AIDS. He only has to catch it from a patient who has it. The dental hygienist who cleans your teeth also cleans the teeth of many others, and a slight slip in hygiene can pass an infection to you. The few cases of AIDS patients have caught from doctors or dentists are only the most sensational part of the problem.

Another problem is that AIDS-infected persons are still selling their blood. Drug abusers sell blood because they need the money, but some homosexuals do it to spread the disease among the general population. Although companies dealing in the collection and sale of blood strenuously deny that infected blood gets through their screening, no test is perfect, and even a small percentage of AIDS-infected blood is dangerous.

Catching AIDS makes headlines. Catching hepatitis, which can also be life-threatening, is not sensational enough to grab headlines, but it's more common because hepatitis is more contagious. Staph infection runs through some hospital wards because it's highly contagious.

Sometimes you have no choice. If you're seriously injured and need emergency surgery, you have to take the risks of surgical errors, AIDS and other infections from transfusions, and being administered the wrong drugs.

Elective surgery is another matter. You have a choice. You also have time to seek other opinions and to balance the risks against the benefits.

There are several types of surgery that are conspicuously overdone in the United States. While any sort of operation may be unnecessary, some are so overprescribed and abused that you should be very careful when a doctor suggests them.

Cesarean section is popular right now. In other Western countries, almost all women still deliver babies the natural way, as they used to in this country. Since about 1970, however, American obstetricians have persuaded patients to have their babies delivered Cesarean, so that today, about 25 percent of babies are delivered this way.

It's hard to understand why American women have supposedly become incapable of having natural vaginal deliveries, unless one looks at the mercenary motive. Cesareans cost at least three times as much as natural deliveries. They're also easier to schedule than natural deliveries, and an obstetrician who takes his Wednesday afternoon golf seriously prefers not to have his game preempted by a patient going into labor.

Hysterectomy is another type of elective and profitable surgery. American women have more hysterectomies than women in other industrialized nations. Again, the only explanation of why American women undergo this surgery so often is the pecuniary motive.

Circumcision is the most commonly performed operation in the United States and is totally useless. The United States is the only Western country in which doctors routinely circumcise baby boys in the name of "prevention." Circumcision is cheap and dirty surgery performed on babies without anesthesia, but it's profitable. At $150 or more apiece, it doesn't take many circumcisions to cover the payments on a Mercedes or pay for a trip to Hawaii.

Plastic or cosmetic surgery is a growth industry, and doctors are finding it lucrative enough to justify advertising for patients. Except for reconstructive surgery after accident or injury, plastic surgery is based on vanity and is really unnecessary. This is why the Internal Revenue Service began disallowing deductions for plastic surgery beginning with the taxable year 1991.

Some doctors are unqualified, practicing plastic surgery without special training by taking advantage of loopholes in the law. In one Arizona case, a doctor without any formal training in plastic surgery opened a plastic surgery practice in partnership with an experienced plastic surgeon, continuing after his partner's death. There were several patient complaints, and the Arizona Board of Medical Examiners moved against him.[2]

Some forms of plastic surgery are also dangerous. Silicon

breast implants have produced unexpected complications for many women who had them inserted, bringing up questions about the basic safety of the procedure. The FDA has challenged the safety of silicon implants.[3] Nevertheless, plastic surgeons performed many silicon implants, patients' welfare being secondary to their ability to pay.

At times, the problem is malpractice, or an incompetent surgeon. One woman won an award of $10 million in compensation for the scarring and excess tissue removed when two surgeons performed a "breast reduction" operation on her.[4]

There are many incompetent doctors out there, and most still escape peer review and discipline. Doctors cover up for each other. Federal investigators found that state medical boards suspended or revoked the licenses of only a few of the physicians presumed to be mentally ill or abusing alcohol or drugs. In one case, a doctor was allowed to become a head of a hospital department despite thirty-two sexual-abuse complaints against him.[5]

The federal government has started a data bank to collect information on doctors who have been sued for malpractice, expelled from a hospital staff, or otherwise disciplined. This is the result of a provision of the Health Care Quality Improvement Act of 1986. The National Practitioner Data Bank, however, is not open to the public, as a result of behind-the-scenes pressure from medical groups.[6] This is in sharp contrast with the computerized records on patients who sue being available to doctors, as we've seen.

The conclusion is clear. It's important to avoid medical treatment, especially surgery, unless absolutely necessary. The side effects and complications are becoming more serious, more unpredictable, and more dangerous.

"Ten Minute Medicine"

Experience has shown that, even in the city, immediate care after an injury can often make the difference between life and death. It can also make the difference between a clean recovery and being maimed. This is why ambulance drivers today are specially trained in emergency medicine. However, the ambulance takes time to arrive, and in some cities the delay, because of traffic or backed-up calls, can be many minutes or even hours. This is why you should be able to administer emergency medicine yourself.

The concept of "ten minute medicine" is simply that if you can keep the victim alive for the ten minutes following the injury, his chances of survival and recovery jump dramatically. A practical way to learn the techniques of "ten minute medicine" is to take a "First Responder" course at a community college. This is typically a forty-hour course, and it requires a textbook and some basic equipment, such as a blood pressure gauge, stethoscope, and first-aid supplies.

If you can afford the extra time and tuition, you should take an advanced course, such as the "Emergency Medical Technician" course, or even the "Paramedic" program. These involve not only classroom work, but hands-on instruction at a local hospital emergency room. If you can't do this yourself, make sure that at least one member of your family or group has done so.

First Aid in Remote Areas

If you're a hiker, hunter, or outdoorsman, you'll need to take care of yourself and your party when professional medical care is hours away. This makes First Responder or similar training vital and also brings a need for specialized supplies. A compact medical kit weighs only a few pounds and should contain several drugs available only by prescription. Among these are:

- Gelfoam, which promotes clotting and helps stop hemorrhage.
- A painkiller, such as Demerol, preferably in injectable form. Pills will do in a pinch.

- A wide-spectrum, powerful antibiotic, such as Keflex, for quick treatment of infections.
- Several plastic bags of Ringer's Lactate, useful for replacing fluids in severe injuries.
- An intravenous kit.

Obtaining these is easier than it might appear. If you have a family doctor whom you've known for years, and who knows you well enough to know that you're not a pill-popper, you can explain your need and ask him or her for prescriptions for small quantities of these drugs. If a member of your group works in health care and has access to these supplies, this member can probably obtain small quantities.

Avoiding Medical Rip-Offs

Modern doctors have developed several sophisticated ways of pyramiding profits and ripping off their patients, apart from prescribing unnecessary surgery. One way is to have a piece of the action in various health care facilities.

If surgery is unavoidable, try to have it in an outpatient clinic, not a hospital. Hospital bills are padded mercilessly, and an aspirin can easily cost two dollars, while a box of tissues costs three or four. A sixteen-ounce bottle of hydrogen peroxide, selling for eighty-five cents in a drugstore, lists at ten dollars on a typical hospital bill. Other charges are similarly jacked-up.[7]

It gets worse. Some hospitals bribe doctors to admit patients into their care. Dr. Arnold Relman, editor of the *New England Journal of Medicine,* has stated flatly that "the doctor is in bed with the hospital." Some hospitals, such as the Simi Valley Adventist Hospital of Simi Valley, California, gave a $25,000 loan to an obstetrician in return for bringing his patients to that hospital. In return, he did not have to repay the loan. Financial incentives such as this one cause doctors to place their patients in the hospital that offers them the best deal, not necessarily the best care for patients. Other types of incentives are cash bonuses, minimum income guarantees, free office space, and free office and medical equipment.[8]

Although it's certain that you'll pay more for medical care during the nineties, you won't necessarily get better care. In fact, you may get worse care and find yourself pressured to consent to more tests, treatments, and operations—not because they're useful, but because they're profitable for doctors and hospitals.

ENDNOTES

1. Michael Waldholz and Walt Bogdanich, "Doctor-Owned Labs Earn Lavish Profits in a Captive Market," *Wall Street Journal* (1 March 1989).
2. David Cannella, "Scottsdale Physician Faces New Complaints," *Arizona Republic* (27 January 1991).
3. "Cosmetic Breast Implants Again Cited as Health Risk," *New York Times* (19 April 1991).
4. "$10 Million Awarded in Breast-Surgery Suit," Associated Press (17 January 1991).
5. "Most Unfit Physicians Still Escape Discipline, Study Reports," United Press (6 June 1986). Judging from recent events, there's no reason to believe that the situation has improved at all.
6. Joe Volz, "Government List of Bad Doctors to be Kept Secret," *Newsday* (2 January 1990).
7. Victor Santoro, *The Rip-off Book* (Port Townsend, Washington: Loompanics, Unlimited, 1986), Vol. 2, 9-11.
8. Fred Bayles and Daniel Q. Haney, "Money, Gifts Used

to Retain Doctors' Loyalty," Associated Press (2 December 1990).

PRIVACY PROTECTION

Do you think that your home is your castle and that what you do on your days off is none of your employer's business? Wrong! Today, there's a hard push by employers to make their employees' private lives their business, under the guise of enforcing law and order and a "drug-free" workplace.

When Congress passed the Privacy Act of 1974, the purpose was to protect citizens from unwarranted probing by government agencies. However, there's no protection against various forms of investigation by private concerns. Recently, Congress passed a law prohibiting polygraph testing by most private employers, but this closes only one approach to privacy invasion. Various public safety employees, employees of security firms, and employees of pharmacies and pharmaceutical firms are still subject to this.

Compulsory drug testing is spreading. An increasing number of companies are using "employee screening questionnaires" to select employees, and private investigators are worming their way into company security programs. All of these threaten your privacy and increase your risk of false accusations.

You still have constitutional rights, but this is only theory. As an employee, you're in a terribly weak position. If you refuse to take a drug test, fill out a questionnaire, or submit to an interrogation, you may ultimately be able to sue and have the case decided in your favor by the U.S. Supreme Court. However, this process always takes years, and "justice delayed is justice denied." In the meantime, what do you do to support yourself and feed your family? This is why refusal is not practical unless you've got another job lined up and can afford to tell your employer what he can do with his test.

Forced Drug Testing

Drug testing of employees began with two premises—that police officers enforcing drug laws ought to be drug-free themselves, and that people working in transportation industries should not be impaired. Drug testing by employers is spreading, and today it affects employees in many occupations, although it's hard to see how a hardware store clerk who smokes marijuana to relax in the evenings endangers public safety.

If you feel that you're safe because you don't do drugs, you're mistaken. There is a definite rate of false positives in drug testing, although the laboratories who provide this service steadfastly deny it. This means that each year, a number of innocent people are denied employment or lose their jobs because of faulty tests. The tolerance most companies allow is a 5-percent false-positive rate, and if you're one of the 5 percent, your employment is in jeopardy.[1]

Nobody can force you to submit a urine sample for drug testing, of course, but in practice it's hard to say "no." If you apply for employment with a company that requires drug testing of all candidates, your refusal means that you lose all chances of being considered for employment. If you're already employed, refusal can jeopardize your job. You may be asked to sign a form at the start of employment stating that you will submit to drug testing whenever your employer deems it suitable, and that violating this agreement means that you lose your job, period. Even without this, there's a lot of informal pressure an employer can put on you. "If you don't use drugs, what are you afraid of?" is the common way of handling any reluctance to submit to testing. In short, employers equate refusal with guilt.

One way of countering the risk of forced drug testing is to obtain a prescription for a tranquilizer from your physician. Simply tell him that you occasionally feel nervous or upset. If you've had a recent death in the family or other real-life event to support your request, take advantage of it to obtain a prescription. Once you have the pills, you need not take them, but keep the bottle on hand in case you ever test positive in a test. If this happens, you simply bring the vial in to show your employer and explain that this may have caused the false positive. You can expect to hear a denial that a tranquilizer could affect the test, but it does happen, and this may save your job.

The form you sign "consenting" to the test should list the drugs with which the testing procedure can react to give a false positive. Read this carefully and be sure you write down everything you've taken within the past week. Ibuprofen can register as marijuana. Cough syrup with codeine will cause a positive for morphine. A simple allergy pill can torpedo your test, and it's wise to make sure that your prospective employer knows if you've taken any.

One defense against hitting a positive is to flush out your system by drinking lots of water and exercise for a day or two before the test. This will tend to dilute your urine—and any substances in it.

A practice to avoid is obtaining a sample of supposedly "clean" urine, which some enterprising individuals sell for as much as twenty bucks per vial. The reason? A urine test also involves measuring the sample's temperature as a safeguard against this trick. The specimen bottle has a liquid crystal thermometer, such as the one made by Doxtech, fixed to the outside with an adhesive strip. The reading must be within the acceptable range, 90.5-98.8°F, for the specimen to be acceptable.[2] In a rigorous test setup, a staffer will even come into the toilet to watch you pee.

A more sinister aspect of drug testing is that the employer can also conduct other tests secretly, such as screening for diabetes, pregnancy, or even HIV. As of early 1991, the

Turner Broadcasting Company and Fortunoff retail stores had announced that tobacco smokers would not be hired and that employees who smoked, even off-duty, would have to quit. The Ford Meter Box Company, of Wabash, Indiana, fired two employees because urine testing revealed traces of nicotine. You have no sure safeguard against this, but you ought to be aware of the possibility. One good piece of news is that, as of this date, Colorado, Kentucky, Oregon, Rhode Island, South Carolina, Tennessee, and Virginia have enacted laws protecting the rights of employees to smoke off the job. Indiana Representative Vernon Smith introduced a bill in the same vein, and nineteen other state legislatures are considering such bills.[3]

Employee Screening Questionnaires

An employee screening questionnaire can be both mystifying and threatening to a job applicant. You sit down to answer a list of two hundred questions, wondering what they have to do with your qualifications for employment, and the uncertainty adds to the anxiety you normally feel when job-hunting. You know that your acceptance depends partly on the answers you provide, and that you may suffer rejection without ever knowing the real reason why.

The reason employers use questionnaires is to save money on preemployment screening. The most reliable way to check out an applicant is by conducting a background investigation and checking references, including former employers. This takes time, and time is money. A quicker—though dirty—way is to use a questionnaire that explores the applicant's attitudes, and theoretically measures his potential behavior.

Questionnaire Theory

When you take such a test you'll find a list of questions that you can answer with a "yes" or "no" or a multiple-choice. The questions deal with your history of alcohol and drug use, if any, and some will ask you outright if you've ever used drugs, stolen from an employer, or been convicted of a traffic violation. Others will deal with your attitudes towards employers and towards people who use drugs, steal, or abuse alcohol.

The theory behind the questions is simple—and simple-minded. To be acceptable, you must be fairly honest but have low tolerance of forbidden behaviors. You must also have a punitive attitude towards those who break the rules. Finally, you must not appear to be perfect yourself. All questionnaires contain "control" questions relating to small violations, under the theory that nobody's perfect, and anyone who denies ever having broken the rules is "faking good."[4] Let's see how this works out in practice.

Taking the Test

The instructions will probably tell you to work through the questions quickly, giving the first answer that comes into your mind. That's exactly what you don't want to do! Always think about the question and its implications before answering, and always consider what sort of answer will improve your prospects of getting the job.

Passing these tests is mostly common sense. At the start, look over the questions before answering any and you'll easily spot the control questions dealing with minor failings. Admit the small stuff, deny the big no-nos, and you'll pass with flying colors. As you scan the test, watch for similar questions. They're designed to spot inconsistencies.

Also watch for questions dealing with your personal tastes and behavior. You want to project an image of vanilla ice cream—a basically happy person with a good home life, a team player, and an extrovert. You don't play chess or read many books or do anything else that could make it appear that you prefer your own company.

If you admit to flagrant violations such as felonies, you're out, of course. If you show tolerance of forbidden behavior, you're also suspect. If you admit that many of your friends use drugs, that identifies you as a risk.

In answering these questions, you can admit to having stolen small items, such as stationery and objects of small dollar value, from former employers. You can also admit to being merely average in honesty. You may also admit to having tried marijuana once or twice, as a teenager, but state that you no longer use it.

You should also answer that most of the people you know are honest, and that few people steal, cheat on taxes, or commit other crimes. You should also show a harsh and punitive attitude towards those who commit infractions. If asked about what should be done with a long-time employee who has stolen, the answer should be to arrest or fire him. Likewise with the employee caught using drugs on the job.

Polygraph Testing

The theory behind polygraph testing is even simpler than the theory behind questionnaires: liars feel stress, and the polygraph detects the physical signs of stress. A set of pens scribes lines on a moving roll of chart paper. The reason the polygraph works very poorly is that people undergoing the test also feel stress, whether they're truthful or not. A job applicant wired up to a machine feels stress, and so does a person accused of a crime.

As we've seen, you're unlikely to have to undergo a polygraph test unless you're applying for a sensitive job, but police and employers may ask you to take such a test to help clear yourself of suspicion during an investigation. Basically, they use the polygraph because they're lazy. A full-scale investigation is costly and takes time and effort, and they hope that the polygraph will uncover the guilty party quickly.

If you're ever faced with this problem, the first point to decide is whether you really have to take the test. You have the right to refuse, even in a criminal investigation, and the best choice is to turn down the request. If this is impossible, learn how to beat the test.

The main fact to remember is that the polygraph is not really a "lie detector." It cannot uncover lies. It only records physical signs of anxiety and stress. This is why the people who administer such tests use them for intimidation, rather than scientific lie detection. The entire program is designed to build anxiety and convince the subject that every corner of his personality is open to scrutiny and resistance is useless. Many of the successes upon which polygraph technicians build are instances when the subject breaks down and confesses. Always remember that most polygraph testing is based on bluff. Let's scrutinize exactly how a polygraph technician will try to bluff you.

The process begins with a pretest interview, during which the tester will try to convince you that the polygraph is infallible and that your task is to convince him that you're innocent. He'll read a list of questions and ask you if you have any problems with them. The real purpose of this session is to build anticipation and anxiety. Next, the technician will wire you up to the machine and ask you the questions.

Some zany and creative polygraph technicians try to bluff their subjects right at the outset. A favorite trick is to have the subject pick a card and then direct him to answer "no" to all questions regarding the card he picked. The technician watches the chart and always identifies the correct card, because he used a "force deck," in which all fifty-two cards are alike!

It's normal to show a reaction when asked an accusatory question. "Did you murder your wife?" and "Have you ever molested children?" will send your blood pressure to the ceiling. One way to control your reaction is to take a tranquilizer before arriving at the session. You can expect the technician to ask you during the pretest interview if you've taken any drugs or alcohol in the past twenty-four hours, and you simply deny it.

The thumbtack in the shoe trick is an old one, and it is

one way of boosting your reactions to noncritical questions and confusing the technician. You can attain the same results by holding your breath for a few seconds or tightening your muscles.

The critical part is the post-test interview, which is the real *interrogation*. The technician will go over some of the questions with you, making statements such as, "The chart shows a reaction to this question." Note that he's not actually calling you a liar. He's just beating you over the head with doubt, working on the implied assumption that it's your job to prove yourself innocent by convincing him. It's all bluff. He may be so bold as to tell you, "The polygraph can't be wrong, because it's only an instrument recording your reactions."[5]

Never deviate from your answers in response to these bluffs. Keep in mind that the technician is not telling you that he has positive proof that your response was untrue, but merely that the chart shows a "reaction." This is smoke and mirrors, designed to coerce a confession. Keep your cool and stick to your story. One way of dealing with this bluff is to answer something like this:

"That question really worried me, because a couple of years ago I read a magazine article about someone who was asked the same thing on a polygraph exam, and he lost the job because of his answer."

Another way, in this case applicable to a question regarding alcohol use, is: "My uncle's been an alcoholic all his life, and he just died of liver disease last week."

There are many variations, according to the question:

- "A couple of months ago I stopped to help at a bad traffic accident, and it was the goriest thing I ever saw. The cop said the driver was drunk."
- "My parents were divorced."
- "My wife's brother is gay, and he died of AIDS a couple of months ago."

- "My oldest sister was badly hurt by a child molester a couple of years before I was born."

If you keep your cool, you can counter any bluff a polygraph technician presents, and you'll even be able to bluff your way through the post-test interview. Keeping cool is important in interviews and interrogations, which we'll discuss next.

Interviews and Interrogations

What's the difference between an interview and an interrogation? For the purposes of this discussion, the difference is very simple. An interview is a session to discuss a prospect, such as a job or promotion. An interrogation is a question-and-answer session when you're under suspicion and is more threatening.

There are competent and incompetent interviewers. The incompetent works through a list of questions and records your answers. The skilled interviewer is also an actor, able to feign emotions and change moods to provoke a reaction from you. He begins with small talk and routine questions to condition you to answering. This also provides an opportunity to observe you when you're not stressed out by tough questions. The interviewer may feign anger, or more likely disbelief, using nonverbal language. The interviewer may try to bluff you by raising an eyebrow or repeating a key word from your answer. Keep your cool, and reaffirm your statement.

The legitimate purpose of a preemployment interview is to explore your qualifications for the job. Unfortunately, some interviewers abuse their powers and overestimate their abilities. They feel that they can effectively probe your psyche and evaluate how honest you are by asking an adroit series of questions.

Some specialize in trick questions, or questions designed

to put you on the spot, such as asking you to describe the former employer you liked the least, or to describe your greatest weakness. Questions such as these put you in a corner because you cannot reasonably state that you liked all of your former employers equally or that you have no weaknesses. Dealing with these questions requires fast footwork. You can state that the employer you liked the least was one who did not allow you enough initiative in doing your job, and that your greatest weakness is an impatience to get the job done. That way, you turn negatives into positives.[6]

Some interviewers are very bold, especially if they've got a degree in psychology. They may feel justified in asking you probing personal questions, including loaded ones such as, "At what age did you start to masturbate?" At this point, you might simply state that it's none of their business. Resist the temptation to try to be clever by pointing out the logical fallacy behind the question. Don't reply by stating that it was not yet established that you ever did masturbate. This sort of interviewer has an ego problem, a feeling that he is above other people, which entitles him to ask them probing and demeaning personal questions. If you challenge his cleverness and shatter his self-image, you may win the battle but lose the war. He'll find reasons not to recommend you for the job.

In preemployment interviews, follow the same principles as in handling questionnaires. Admit to small faults, state that most people you know are honest, and state that offenders deserve punishment. In admitting faults, always include how you learned from your mistakes. It's also okay to admit that you did not like a former employer, but emphasize that the reason you did not was that this employer was so poor compared to the splendid fellows for whom you've worked most of your career. An interesting twist in this line of bullshit is to say that the reason you disliked this previous employer is that he used drugs, which you feel do not belong in the workplace. That scores a plus for you.

As with questionnaires, use common sense. If the interviewer asks you if you ever knew anyone who used drugs, denial would be totally unconvincing in today's society unless you've lived all your life in a small town in Utah. You can state, though, that a college roommate used drugs, and that when you discovered this you moved out. Your reason for moving out can be that if police ever raided him, they might think the drugs were partly or totally yours.

An *interrogation* is quite different. If you have ever felt pressured during a preemployment interview, that was merely a pale shadow of the pressure you'll feel when you're under suspicion. This is especially true when you're being interrogated by an employer or private investigator. Police must give you the "Miranda Warning," to advise you that you have the right to remain silent and the right to an attorney. Private investigators are under no such restraint, and they can lean on you very hard.

Many investigators believe that they can tell when a subject is lying. They maintain that the liar licks his lips, covers his mouth, scratches his face and neck, crosses his arms, evades questions, does not look at the interrogator, and so on. These signs of nervousness, according to them, are signs of guilt.[7]

Defending yourself against interrogation depends on whether you're guilty or innocent, because the tactics will vary somewhat. If you're really guilty, and you know that they have the evidence, take advantage of your Miranda rights, remain silent, and get a lawyer. Remember that you have the right to remain silent, avoiding incriminating yourself, and the right to an attorney, whether the interrogator so advises you or not. Make them work for their conviction. Never give it away free by confessing, unless you can obtain a real deal.

You can expect both verbal and nonverbal coercion. Threats, offers of a deal, and other verbal techniques are fairly direct and give you a fair chance of making a decision regarding the merits of the offer. Nonverbal techniques include invading your personal space, with the interrogator sliding his chair close to you to produce a feeling of intimidation. By getting closer when you answer in a way he doesn't like and backing away when you deliver an answer that pleases him, the interrogator gets you "mentally programmed to cooperate."[8]

Be prepared for trick questions. An interrogator may use the "ghost witness" technique and ask you, "What would you say if I told you that a witness saw you there?" Keep your wits and remember that this is a "what if" question, not a statement of fact, and that you need only repeat that you were, indeed, where you said you were.

Private security officers can be very nasty and very persuasive. Unfettered by Miranda, and holding the threat of dismissal over employees, they can be very bold with their accusations. One retail chain's security officers allegedly bullied confessions of theft from at least three hundred former employees, who later filed a federal lawsuit. Using threats of arrest and exposure, security officers had forced employees to sign confessions, and make "restitutions" of many thousands of dollars.[9]

Preparation

A good way to learn how to tell a convincing story is to watch those who earn their livings by convincing others. Observe salesmen and politicians closely, noting their different styles, so that you can decide which style suits your personality best. You may want to do some close-up research, and one of the best ways is to make the rounds of automobile dealers and watch their salesmen try to sell you a car. Because you're only window-shopping, you'll be able to concentrate on their techniques. Make notes after each encounter and adopt the techniques you feel will work best for you.

The big secret to coping with interviews is preparation by rehearsal. Plan and rehearse your answers in advance to minimize surprise and polish your delivery. The best part about preemployment interviews is that you can use employers' resources against them. Apply for jobs you don't really want, just to have the opportunity to take interviews. You can even make a game of it, applying for jobs for which you're totally unqualified, to see how far you can get before being exposed. This may require telling lies for survival, which we'll study next.

ENDNOTES

1. Martin Yate, *Knock 'em Dead,* 1991 Edition (Boston: Bob Adams, Inc.,1991), 203-205.
2. Available from Doxtech, Inc., 4000 Easton Drive #10, Bakersfield, CA 93309.
3. *Smokers' Advocate,* Vol. 2, Issue 5, (May 1991).
4. David Thoreson Lykken, *A Tremor in the Blood* (New York: McGraw-Hill, 1981), 199-201.
5. Ibid., 205-215.
6. Martin John Yate, *Knock 'em Dead* (Boston: Bob Adams Inc., 1987), 99-150.
7. Daniel D. Evans, "10 Ways to Sharpen Your Interviewing Skills," *Law and Order* (August 1990): 90-95.
8. Ibid., 91.
9. Associated Press (3 September 1990).

FOR FURTHER READING

1. Charles Clifton, *Deception Detection: Winning the Polygraph Game* (Boulder, Colorado: Paladin Press, 1991).

TELLING LIES FOR SURVIVAL

The threat to your privacy is real, and it's increasing as interviewers and other information seekers develop more sophisticated techniques of prying information from you. Although investigative techniques have evolved greatly, the first and basic one is still obtaining information from the subject himself. Keep this in mind and you'll learn to think cautiously during any interview or interrogation, and you'll avoid giving away anything you don't absolutely have to.

There are legitimate reasons for telling lies. A person with an embarrassing past who is trying to straighten out his life would not want a prospective employer to know about a prison record. A divorce may be worth hiding, even in today's enlightened era. In some situations, you may want to pass for several years younger than your true age. If you have to shade the truth, there are some simple rules to follow:

- First, try to relax. Keep in mind that nobody's perfect, and that many people feel nervous when under investigation. Other innocent people might fare even worse than you.
- Get your story straight in your own mind and stick to it. If you know you're correct, never change your story. Any contradictions or inconsistencies count against you.
- Tell your story once, then shut up. You may answer

questions if they pertain to something you did not cover in your first account, but do not fall into the trap of going over the same points again and again. An interrogator knows that when a subject is asked to repeat his account there will inevitably be some slight discrepancies in detail, and he uses these as leverage to convince the subject that he knows he's lying. This intimidation tactic sometimes forces a confession.

- When you speak, look straight at the interrogator. Failing to meet his gaze or shifting your eyes will count against you.
- Always pause before you answer, giving yourself an extra second to think. If you're unsure of your answer, have the interviewer repeat the question.
- State your story in clear and unequivocal terms. If you're denying guilt, say simply, "I didn't do it." If you're stating an alibi, say simply, "I was there from eight to ten," or a similar statement, in clear and unequivocal terms. The reason is that evasive answers, or hedging, sound suspicious. Some interrogators are into linguistic analysis, and a basic rule is that if you don't say it, it didn't happen or it's not true.
- Don't misstate any facts the interviewer can easily check. You have to use good judgment on this point. A private employment interviewer probably won't check employment in the distant past or education, unless the job pays very well indeed. The government will check everything, especially when a security clearance is involved.
- Don't invent anything just to avoid admitting ignorance. If you don't know the answer to a question, say so. Anything you invent to cover ignorance—or gaps in your original statement— may return to haunt you.
- Never volunteer information. Any additional details

you provide to reinforce your case may only provoke more questions.

- Be prepared for the disguised interview after the session's ended. The interviewer turns off the tape recorder, or puts on his jacket and invites you to lunch. This is to get you off your guard, in the hope that you'll be more revealing.

SURVEILLANCE SMARTS

In discussing surveillance, it's important to remember that the most successful surveillance agents are the most inconspicuous. The Hollywood stereotype of a trench-coated figure with upturned collar and snap-brim hat is too blatant. So are two men in a car. For stationary surveillance, known colloquially as a "stakeout," a wino sprawled on the sidewalk is just as likely to be a stakeout agent as not. Likewise, a middle-aged woman with a string shopping bag attracts little attention in most locales and is a good choice for a tail. She has the advantage of being able to stop and look into a store window whenever you stop, without attracting much attention.

Some favorite personas adopted by surveillance agents are street vendors, delivery men, Santa Claus in season, and service personnel, such as window washers and street workers. These fit into most locales, and they attract little attention because most people take them for granted.

How to Tail

The most important aspect of moving surveillance, or "tailing," is the subject's level of awareness. Many people go about their daily travels almost like sleepwalkers, aware only of potential dangers such as traffic hazards, and not taking close and careful looks at people around them. This is why muggers do so well. Victims are often unaware of the danger signs.

The second most important point is remaining inconspicuous, so that if your target is unaware of you, he remains unaware as you follow him. Remaining inconspicuous means fitting into the locale and doing nothing to call attention to yourself.

Distance and appearance both affect your camouflage. The farther you remain from your target, the less likely he'll be to notice you. If you dress the part, you'll look as if you "belong" in the area. A black man with diddly-bop hat and carrying a large radio would not fit into certain locales. Likewise, a white man wearing an expensive three-piece suit looks out of place in a ghetto.

There are several types of tails. The close tail is for when it's imperative not to lose the subject, even if he becomes aware of the surveillance. The loose tail is for when remaining undiscovered is the main priority. The spot-check is an extreme type of tail, suitable for subjects who take the same route each day and when being spotted would be a major disaster. This involves picking the subject up at home, for example, following him for two or three blocks, and breaking off surveillance. The next day, you wait for him where you left off, follow him for another short distance, and discontinue the tail. Eventually, you'll discover where he goes each day.

The longer you follow your subject, the more important it becomes to change your appearance. This doesn't mean putting on a false mustache or beard, but breaking your profile by donning or doffing a hat, coat, or jacket. It also helps to have more than one person tailing and to change positions regularly, so that the same person isn't always closest to the subject.

How to Check for a Tail

There are many ways to check for tails, some of which are obvious, and others of which are subtle. The type you use depends on whether or not you're willing to let those tailing you know that you're suspicious.

A good inconspicuous way to check for a tail is to use a lure. This is dropping something that the tail will have to pick up and watching to see if he does. To remain inconspicuous, it's important not to make it obvious that you're watching. Dropping a piece of paper is an old trick, and an experienced trailer won't fall for it. If you're being tailed by a team, the closest ones will stick close to you and leave it to "tail-end Charlie" to pick up the paper. To make this work, you have to be more subtle and structure the situation properly.

One way to do this requires a subway or bus. You wait for the subway or bus to arrive, while sitting on a bench reading a newspaper. When it arrives, you put the newspaper down on the bench next to you and board the bus or train, taking a position from which you can watch the bench as you pull out. Anyone who retrieves your newspaper will be immediately obvious, and you can keep an eye on him as he boards after you. This is important, as he may make contact with another member of the tailing team, if there is one. Never forget, though, that your tail may be female. The other possibility is that a person tailing you will wait until you're gone before going for the lure. This could mean that person considers the lure more important than you. More likely, it means there's more than one person tailing you. At least you get rid of one tail, making it a little easier to spot the others.

If no public transport is available, there are other ways of checking for tails by using a lure. One is to drop a package of cigarettes or candy into a wastebasket, or even onto the sidewalk, just before going into a diner or restaurant from which you can watch who stops to retrieve it.

Another way of checking for tails is to go down a street with little traffic, because this makes it hard for followers to blend in with the crowd. This works while driving as well as afoot. In rural areas, choosing a lightly traveled road will do the same for you. An excellent way is to go up a road with switchbacks in mountainous country. Each segment offers a good observation point to scan the road below.

Vary your schedule and route each day to make a spot-check difficult. If you're predictable, you set yourself up for a tail, mugging, or other nasty event. If you're truly security-conscious, don't tell anyone your daily schedule, to make it difficult for anyone to predict where you'll be at any time.

Informers and Undercover Agents

Police use of informers is a growing danger to American freedom, because it enables surveillance of people who have committed no crime but are merely under suspicion. If you become known as a weapons collector or as a "survivalist," you may also fall under scrutiny.

This ties in with keeping a low profile. The other aspect to watch is to be careful of your associates and confidants. If you tell anyone of any illegal or marginal activity of yours, you open up another potential leak. This person may tell another, and word may reach an undercover agent or informer.

PHYSICAL SAFETY

Crime is on almost everyone's mind, and in most urban areas the reality justifies the concern. Even suburban locales are often infested with property crimes.

Violent vs. Nonviolent Crime

Burglary and auto theft are far more common than rape, robbery, and murder. Most street hoods prefer to take what they want by stealth, not force. This is why you have to use different ways of defending yourself.

The Role of the Police

Don't expect too much from the police. Many people misunderstand what the police can do because they take literally what they see on TV cop shows.

Unfortunately, the police can't do much to protect you. They can't be everywhere at once, and lawbreakers try to operate when police aren't around. Unlike what you see in motion pictures and TV dramas, police officers very rarely interrupt a crime in progress. The police usually arrive to take a report after it's over and the suspect has fled. Police officers become very casual about taking reports.

If, for example, you find your car missing, don't be surprised if the officer who comes to take the report isn't at all excited about it. Don't feel offended if he's obviously bored. Having your car stolen may be the worst thing that's happened to you this year, but the officer probably takes several such reports a day. He is also aware that some people have had their vehicles stolen because of stupidity, such as leaving the key in the lock. He also knows that some vehicle thefts involve insurance fraud. The U.S.-Mexico border, for example, offers a route for fraud artists, and some people drive their cars to Mexico, sell them, and report them stolen upon return. Likewise with burglaries. Cops know that even in genuine burglaries some people are tempted to pad the value of what was stolen to collect more from the insurance company.

"Clearance rates," the rates of solving crimes, are low for property crimes. The police do care that more than 1.5 million vehicles are stolen each year, but they can't drop everything if someone steals yours. You may even have to report a burglary by telephone, because they won't send an officer. This is the policy with some "progressive" police departments, when command-level officers admit that most burglaries don't get solved anyway and prefer to apply manpower to other problems.

The lesson is clear: you must protect your own property, because the police won't. The first step is to observe common-sense precautions, such as keeping your car and home locked, keeping especially valuable items in a safe vault, and not carrying more cash than you actually need for immediate use.

A common mistake is to carry almost no cash, instead relying on a wallet full of credit cards or a checkbook. Many people don't realize that check and credit card fraud are rampant, and that a street-smart criminal can loot your checking account or line of credit before you're even aware that anything is wrong. Losing your credit cards or checkbook is even more serious than losing the cash in your wallet.[1]

Violent Crime

This has always been with us, and it appears to be getting worse. The problem is not the crime rate, which bobbles up and down with each year's survey, but with our means of coping with crime. Today we are ineffective, and this problem kicks back at us with two-headed viciousness.

Not only are clearance rates dropping for serious crimes such as homicide, but our prisons are crowded with violators, making early-release programs mandatory. A sentence of ten years does not, in most cases, mean that the convicted felon will spend the next ten years behind bars. Instead, he'll get time off for good behavior, work-release, early release, and perhaps even parole, if he's there long enough for the parole board to hear his case. Only the most extraordinarily vicious or notorious convicts serve their entire sentences.

The truly objectionable part of the criminal justice system is the hard-core cadre of moral revisionists who appear to blame the victim. If you get mugged on the subway, these people will tell you breezily that "that's life in the big city." If you get mugged while jogging in Central Park, they'll say that you ought to know better than to go jogging in Central Park. The worst bureaucratic manifestation of this has hit the New York City Police Department, which now has a "Bias Crimes Unit." This detail investigates crimes that have a racial or ethnic aspect, such as the defacing of a synagogue or an attack on a black by people wearing white sheets. When the young lady jogger was attacked in Central Park, the unit decided that this was not its domain, perhaps because the victim was white. The black teenager shot to death in Bensonhurst, on the other hand, became the accredited victim of a bias crime.

The Arizona legislature recently defeated a "hate crimes" bill, which would have imposed extra penalties for crimes against ethnic people or others who aspire to "minority" status, such as homosexuals. The net effect of such laws is to send a message that attacking mainstream people is less wrong, because it carries lesser penalties.

The second part of the problem is defense against crime. If a mugger attacks you, don't expect the police to rescue you. As with property crimes, the police take a report.

You're likely to be alone when a mugger strikes, but if you try to defend yourself, you may become open to both criminal and civil charges.

In many cities, carrying a concealed weapon is illegal. This applies even to nonlethal electronic stun guns and spray-can weapons. In some cities such as New York, mere possession is a crime, and you cannot buy one on the open market. The bad guys, however, appear to have no procurement problem and easily obtain firearms and other weapons.

Using any weapon against an attacker sets you up for a criminal complaint. Never mind that you were just riding the subway on your way home from work, and that the attacker was trying to mug you. This is especially true if the attacker is a minority group member and you're Caucasian. Don't expect any sympathy from the police or the media. You'll find the media labeling you as a "vigilante," "racist," or worse. You may find yourself wondering if the district attorney's real job is making the streets and subways safe for muggers.

If you're a minority group member yourself, make the most of it. The media won't be able to accuse you of racism if you blow away a minority mugger. In fact, there have been several recent justifiable shootings by minority group members, and they've gotten little publicity. If you're carrying an illegal weapon, though, you'll probably face criminal charges.

Criminal charges are only the good news. A civil suit can follow. The attorney for the suspect shot and paralyzed by Bernhardt Goetz is suing Goetz for 50 million dollars. Even being unarmed may not help you. If, for example, you don't carry a banned weapon but are skilled enough with your fists to overcome your attacker, you're not necessarily in the clear. An enterprising lawyer may get you in civil court for using more force than necessary, especially if your attacker suffers a permanent injury.

Some people take all of this to heart and, when confronted by a mugger, will simply hand over their wallets. Frankly, this often saves them from injury. Most attackers only want money and won't cause more trouble than necessary to obtain what they want. Others, however, enjoy hurting people. When you comply with the mugger's demands, you're betting your life he only wants your money. The occasional "thrill killer" won't let you walk away if you hand over your wallet to save your skin, because he also wants your skin.

Another problem arises when the victim is compliant, because it's bad psychology. Giving in to the mugger reinforces his behavior, because it shows him that he will continue to get what he wants by threatening people. You can hand over your wallet and walk away with a whole skin, thinking that you've solved the problem. Actually, you're passing the problem on to the next victim. Realistically, the person who mugs you does so only because previous victims passively encouraged him by not resisting, thereby reinforcing his predatory behavior.

Whether to resist or not has to be your decision, because you're the one facing the immediate risk. It's not an easy decision, because it's a trade-off. If you comply and hand over your wallet, the police may or may not apprehend the mugger later. Meanwhile, he's free to victimize others. Resistance can get you hurt or killed. If you bring his criminal career to an abrupt end, you'll not only be saving yourself a loss, but you'll be serving society as well. You'll be able to go home satisfied with another job well done.

Hostage

An unlikely but terrifying prospect is being taken hostage by a criminal interrupted during a robbery. It's even less likely that you'll be taken hostage by terrorists unless you do a lot of foreign travel. Your plight is the same, whoever takes you hostage.

If you're a hostage you have two dangers to fear—the

hostage-takers and the police. Hostage-takers may harm you because they don't like you or to enforce their demands. Police may harm you during a rescue attempt if they mistake you for a terrorist or criminal. You also might simply get caught in the cross fire.

Survival depends on your blending in with other hostages. You don't want to attract attention from the hostage-taker, which can give him a reason to select you for execution as a show of force. Avoid eye contact with hostage-takers, and speak only if they speak to you first. Meanwhile, observe them carefully, noting their number, weapons, and locations. If you get an opportunity to escape, this information will be very valuable to police who will debrief you, because it will help them plan a rescue for the other hostages.

If a police squad comes crashing in to rescue you, drop to the floor, cover your eyes and ears, and be still. SWAT officers sometimes use stun grenades, and may order all hostages to lie prone for their own safety. Take them exactly at their word, because they're trained to shoot anyone who stands up. Don't make the mistake of trying to help them by snatching a weapon from one of the hostage-takers. A hostage rescue operation happens very quickly, and officers will reflexively shoot anyone holding a weapon on the assumption that he's a suspect. Keeping a low profile is the key to survival if you become a hostage.

ENDNOTES

1. Burt Rapp, *Credit Card Fraud* (Port Townsend, Washington: Loompanics, 1991). The last part of this book provides specific steps you can take to safeguard your credit cards.

WEAPONS

Defense against criminal attack is a serious problem in many cities because the threat is pervasive. Inner city ghetto areas are "off-limits" to anyone who wants to avoid being mugged, but unfortunately, even what we consider "good" neighborhoods are no longer safe in many cities. Public transport is also a favorite criminal haunt, because street criminals know that middle-class and affluent people travel to work and that not all can afford limousines. Muggers also ambush commuters in public parking lots.

The odds are that if you're attacked you'll need a weapon to defend yourself. Forget about defending yourself with your fists. No matter how adept you are with your fists, you either won't have to use them or you'll be so outnumbered that they'll be useless. That's merely the good news. The bad news is that the street maggot who attacks you will have a weapon.

It's easy to understand this because of the way criminals think. A mugger doesn't want to fight hard to get your wallet. If a single mugger considers attacking you, he'll first size you up, evaluating whether or not he can "take" you easily. This is the way a predator thinks. If he's unarmed, and you look big and tough enough to put up a good fight, he'll pass you by in favor of a more vulnerable target. A little old lady makes a better target because she's less able to put up an effective struggle. If the mugger has a knife or gun, he'll be able to overcome you if you're unarmed.

You may have seen a martial arts expert disarming an armed felon in the movies or on TV. This can work if he's close enough, you're fast and skilled enough, and his reaction time is slow. If you try to disarm a mugger, you're betting your life that you can do it without getting killed. If the mugger is street-smart, he'll keep enough distance between you and his weapon to avoid your disarming him, and he'll order you to toss over your wallet, car keys, or whatever else he wants.

If there's more than one mugger, the odds are impossible. If a mugging team has even basic tactical sense, one will remain in the background, covering you with his weapon, while the other approaches you to get your wallet. If they're armed with knives, they'll split up, approaching you from both sides. You won't even be able to watch both at once, much less fight them.

Nonlethal Weapons

A firearm is often the only way you can even the odds. An aerosol can hasn't got the range, and a knife is a contact weapon, putting you in as much danger as your adversary. Stun guns are also contact weapons, because you have to press the electrodes against the target's body. A club can provide more striking range, but there may not be room to swing it. Unfortunately, cities with the worst crime problems also tend to have the strictest gun control laws. Carrying concealed weapons is illegal, and in many locales, even possession in the home is forbidden. These laws really disarm the honest citizen, because despite federal, state, and local laws, criminals never have trouble obtaining firearms.

Although it's not the purpose of this book to encourage you to break the law, it's only realistic to admit that many feel that "it's better to be tried by twelve than carried by six." Many people will procure and keep an illegal weapon for defense, because weighing the risks shows that being prosecuted is better than being killed.

There's another side to this question. Some people feel that they would be unable to take another person's life, whatever the circumstances. This rules out a firearm but leaves stun guns and chemical sprays. Let's take a quick look at the characteristics of each.

A stun gun is an electronic device, usually drawing from a 9-volt battery, which produces a current as high as 50,000 volts. Manufacturers of some models claim higher voltages. Placing the stun gun's electrodes in contact with the attacker sends a high-voltage charge into his body, stunning him and stopping his attack. Tests have shown that the high-voltage current will penetrate clothing.

That's the theory. The main problem with a stun gun is that you have to be within touching distance of your attacker. If you can reach him, he can reach you. If you're holding a stun gun and he has a knife or club, you're betting your life that you can immobilize him with the stun gun before he can hurt you. Another problem is that if your hands are wet, the high voltage current may also go through your body. A few police officers have reported being shocked by their own stun guns when the suspect's clothing was wet. Finally, the spark that jumps between the electrodes can ignite flammable vapors.

Chemical sprays have longer ranges. Some shoot a stream about fifteen feet. Others shoot cones of mist for an effective range of about six feet. This is far better than a stun gun, but sprays don't work well in crosswinds and are worse than useless if you're downwind from the attacker. The most effective chemical spray is the type using cayenne pepper extract, known as "oleoresin capsicum." A one-second burst will stop almost anyone if directed at the face, because it causes a choking feeling, and the eyelids close from immediate swelling. This is why Cap-Stun and similar brands are quickly taking over the police and correctional markets.[1]

A stun gun or chemical spray is a poor defense against a club or knife, and very inadequate against an assailant armed with a gun. Often, the only effective weapon is a firearm. This is the final solution.

Firearms

If this is your choice, the first step is obtaining one. Getting a gun is harder than buying a stun gun or chemical spray, because federal laws regulate their sale, even in states with few gun laws. If you want a chemical spray, you simply buy one in a state allowing their sale. There's no legal requirement to produce ID. You can even ask a relative or friend living where they're legal to buy one for you and to ship it by package express.

Obtaining a Firearm

Obtaining a firearm in a state with restrictive laws can be a problem. You can still ask a friend or relative in another state to buy one for you and ship it, but if he buys it from a licensed dealer, he'll have to show ID, and the firearm will be traceable to him by the serial number. If ever the police find it after a shooting, investigation will lead to his door.

There's a better way. Federal law still doesn't regulate sales between individuals. Going to a state with no local laws restricting firearms sales allows exploiting this aspect of the law. Newspapers carry classified ads listing firearms offered for sale by private individuals. Paying cash to a private party makes the transaction untraceable and provides a "clean" firearm.

When purchasing a firearm this way, always ask the seller how long he's had the weapon. If he bought it before 1 January 1969, there's no federal paperwork on it. If he bought it since, ask where he bought it. A purchase from a licensed dealer involves a record on the Bureau of Alcohol, Tobacco, and Firearms Form 4473. If he bought it privately the transaction is clean, unless he bought it in a state that requires registration of all firearms sales.

There's yet another way of obtaining an untraceable firearm, because of a glaring weakness in federal firearms laws. A Federal Firearms License (FFL) is fairly easy to obtain and enables you to order firearms directly from a manufacturer or distributor and have them shipped to you across a state line. Obtaining a legal FFL involves a fair amount of paperwork, and your name goes into government files. A forged FFL is another matter. Those involved in organized crime know that forgery of a Federal Firearms License is simple and allows firearms purchases that are practically untraceable. See Appendix A for an explanation of how this works.

The worst way to buy a firearm is through the underground market in a locale that has very restrictive laws. While you may have heard stories of an acquaintance who bought a pistol in a local bar, such firearms may bring more trouble than they're worth. You might feel secure paying cash for a handgun to an individual whom you've never seen before, but the firearm may be "hot." It may be stolen, and it probably has been used in a crime, which is why the owner wants to get rid of it. If you're ever involved in a shooting that results in a police investigation, you may be under suspicion for other crimes.

There's a way out of this problem. If ever you have to shoot someone, tell the police that the firearm is the suspect's. Your story is that suspect got close enough for you to reach the weapon and that he got shot during the struggle for the gun. If in fact you shot him at more than point-blank range, there won't be any powder burns on him, and your story then must be that you wrestled the gun away from the suspect and tried to flee. You had to shoot him because he pursued you, and you were afraid that he had another weapon. If police investigators tie the firearm to another crime, they'll conclude that your attacker was involved in it.

Which Firearm to Choose?

There are several broad classes of firearms, and many types within each class. All have their advantages and drawbacks. You ought to be clear about one major point: your ability to use the firearm is far more important than the type you choose. Don't just pick a superzapper because you've read a favorable write-up in a gun magazine, but select one that you can handle well.

Reliability is the single most important quality your defensive weapon can have. Caliber, magazine capacity, and speed of reloading don't count for much if the firearm fails to operate when you need it. With these points in mind, let's look at the various types you might consider.

Shotgun

The shotgun is one of the more powerful firearms in common use. The normal caliber for use against two-legged wolves is 12-gauge. The advantages of the shotgun are high power and very limited range, which can be important in a built-up area.

Range depends on the load. A slug is a heavy chunk of lead shaped to fit the shotgun's barrel, and it provides the ability to hit a human-size target at ranges up to about one hundred yards. The heavy slug will smash though a car door, interior wall, and through furniture. This can also be excessive penetration, especially if you open fire inside an apartment house.

No. 8 birdshot has a much shorter range, because the smaller projectiles have ballistic performance inferior to slugs. In practical terms, a charge of No. 8 birdshot comes out of the barrel in a stream about two-thirds of an inch in diameter, but the pattern quickly spreads. At ranges of ten feet or less, the charge will blow a neat hole in a target, but at greater ranges the individual projectiles spread, and lose velocity quickly. With a cylindrical bore shotgun, at thirty feet there isn't enough power left to go through both sides of an interior wall.

The shotgun is a liability if you're using buckshot and the range is greater than ten yards. Beyond this range, the pattern expands so that some pellets will miss a human target. If there are innocent bystanders in the background, they may be hit.

Rifle

A commonly held belief about rifles is that they're exclusively long-range weapons, unsuitable for close defense. Gun writers who should know better spread this fiction, to the detriment of both police and law-abiding civilians. The only advantages of a handgun are light weight and concealability. These are important if you must carry a handgun concealed on your person all day, but there's a trade-off. As we'll see in the section on handguns, they sacrifice power and accuracy.

A rifle is a powerful weapon, often able to inflict a lethal injury with one shot at ranges up to several hundred yards. At close range, a rifle can produce a devastating wound, and in a pinch will serve as a club. Bringing a rifle butt down on your target's head or neck produces a stunning blow and can even be lethal.

Two common criticisms of rifles for urban use are overpenetration and excessive range. The rifle fires a single projectile, which means that if your aim is correct, you won't have to worry about a spreading pattern covering an area larger than your target at long ranges. If you hit your target, you won't have to worry about endangering innocent persons, and hitting your target is easier with a shoulder weapon than with a handgun. This is because you support the weapon with both hands and your shoulder instead of only one or both hands.

This isn't just theory. A famous gun battle on the streets of Miami, Florida, proved the value of a rifle in urban combat. On Saturday, 11 April 1986, eight agents of the FBI caught up with two bank robbery and murder suspects. The suspects resisted arrest, and one, a former paratrooper and a skilled shot, was armed with a Ruger Mini-14. Before FBI gunfire finally brought him down, he shot and killed two agents and wounded five more. The shoot-out took place on a residential street, and at least 140 rounds were fired, yet not one bystander was hit. The suspect with the rifle wasn't concerned about hitting innocent people, but he was a determined fighter and a good marksman. FBI agents mostly used handguns, and most of their shots missed. It was only when one agent opened fire with a shotgun that the battle turned decisively against the suspects.

What caliber should you choose? If you already have a rifle, use that, unless it's chambered for an exotic caliber for which ammo is hard to find. Also avoid the temptation to play macho man. You don't need a superpowerful caliber, such as a .460 Weatherby Magnum, unless you're hunting elephants. If you have a superpowerful gun, your wife or other members of your group may not be able to shoot it.

What you do need is a rifle using ammo that's easy to find, such as calibers .30-'06, .308 Winchester, .243 Winchester, .223 Remington, or .30-30 Winchester. All of these calibers are powerful enough for use against human targets. All are intrinsically accurate beyond 100 yards. The .30-30 is a fairly short-range cartridge with an effective range of about 150 yards, but the others can be effective to well over 300 yards in average hands. These are conservative figures, and skilled marksmen have scored hits at longer ranges.

The type of rifle is very important. If your rifle is your only firearm, always choose a semiauto, because you may have to open fire on multiple close-in attackers, and the semiauto requires only a pull on the trigger for each shot. Semiautos are slightly less accurate than bolt-action rifles, but you have to trade off accuracy for firepower. If you have a handgun for close-in defense, you can use your rifle for long-range shots, and safely choose a bolt-action. If in doubt, choose the semiauto because most gunfights take place at close ranges anyway.

An important accessory for your rifle is a sling. It doesn't have to be fancy, and the most cost-effective sling is nylon webbing because it's sturdy and inexpensive. Nylon doesn't rot from moisture or crack from dryness the way leather does.

The sling serves two purposes. One is as a carrying

strap. The other is to help steady the rifle while firing. A sling can make a tremendous difference when firing from the standing, sitting, or kneeling positions.

Handgun

Tons of ink and paper have been wasted discussing handgun "stopping power." The reason for the problem is that handguns are design compromises, trading off power for light weight and small size. Handguns are more concealable than shoulder weapons, but less powerful and harder to shoot accurately. This is because a handgun is fired with one or both hands. The least accurate way is to use only one hand, but this may be necessary if your other hand is occupied. Unless you're a fairly proficient shot, you'll find that you can hit a human target only at close range with one hand.

Which caliber? It's up to you. A smaller caliber, such as the .22 Long Rifle, is not very powerful, but ammunition is cheap. This is important, because practice makes perfect, and the more practice you can afford, the better you'll become. It's also important to remember that several small bullets cause as much or more destruction as a single large one.

Some calibers, such as the .41 and .44 Magnums, are simply too powerful for comfortable shooting by most people. Ignore the "experts" who claim that anyone, with the proper training, can learn to shoot any caliber. What they really mean is instruction at their shooting school, which can easily cost five hundred dollars for five days, not counting travel and lodging.

Revolver or Auto?

Revolvers are very different from auto pistols in design and operation, but it's possible to become a deadly shot with either one. Revolvers usually cost less than autos but are somewhat more delicate and sensitive to rough use. Autos hold more ammunition, and some 9mm pistols have magazines holding as many as twenty rounds. Revolvers hold five or six cartridges, depending on the model, except for those chambered for .22 Long Rifle, some of which hold as many as nine. Revolvers are also slower to reload, because it's necessary to remove fired cases from the chambers to make room for fresh cartridges.

The "average" shoot-out consumes only between two and three rounds, which means you should not feel hopelessly outclassed if you have a six-shot revolver. Defending yourself against multiple attackers, though, will require more. The reverse side of the coin is that you should not feel invulnerable if you have an auto pistol with a large magazine. If you get into a gunfight with several assailants, you'll probably get shot to death before you can empty your pistol, unless you use proper tactics.

Auto pistols tend to be flatter and more compact than revolvers of similar calibers. The auto pistol's mechanism absorbs some of the recoil, making it somewhat more pleasant to fire. Revolvers are somewhat simpler to learn to operate, but some shooters find them less accurate than autos because of the longer trigger pull when firing double-action. Firing a revolver single-action, cocking the hammer for each shot, is very slow in the context of a gunfight. Autos cock themselves when they cycle.

Stock Angle

Stock or grip angle is one of the most important features of a handgun. The reason is that a handgun, revolver or auto, is a very personal weapon, and you should be able to point it as you do your index finger. This is contrary to the teachings of those who stress using the sights, but unfortunately, real-life shoot-outs tend to take place in poor light, not on a well-lit target range. You can't easily see the sights, and you have to shoot by feel. In an emergency, you depend on what you can do instinctively.

The grip angle should be such that the handgun points naturally at your target, without a tendency to point higher or lower. You can check the handgun for proper fit to your hand by holding it down at your side (empty, of course!), looking at a spot across the room, and closing your eyes. Bring the pistol up to where you feel it's aiming at your target, and open your eyes to see how close you actually came. Do this several times to be sure. Now try this with several handguns. The one which is closest to your intended aiming point when you open your eyes is the one that points most naturally for you. This is the one which will most naturally be on target when the light is too poor to see the sights clearly.

Learning to Shoot

As important as the hardware itself is skill in the firearm's use and the choice of tactics. Bad tactics can nullify the advantages of excellent weapons, while good tactics enable the defender with a modest arsenal to pull through. For your own safety, learn to use your firearm.

Learning to use it means more than aiming and pulling the trigger. You should be able to load and unload the firearm without looking, because you may have to fight for your life in dim light. You should also practice clearing malfunctions, and this is true of both auto pistols and revolvers, which can also jam.

Jam-clearing drills should be reflexive, because you won't have time to stop and think when you're fighting for your life. You should practice the tap-jack-bam drill with an empty gun, to get it right every time. Most auto pistol jams will clear with this drill. The first step is to tap the bottom of the magazine hard to make sure it's seated. The next is to jack the slide, which will remove any dud or jammed round and replace it with a fresh one. The final step is "bam," pulling the trigger.

Sometimes the jam is more serious and difficult to clear. If the pistol still doesn't work after the tap-jack-bam drill, remove the magazine to let any stuck cases drop free. Then jack the slide at least twice and replace the magazine.

Finally, work the slide to insert a fresh round and pull the trigger to fire.

You should learn how to clean and maintain your weapon and have the necessary tools and supplies on hand. You might also consider keeping a few spare parts, because some small parts occasionally break. An extra firing pin, a spare set of springs, and a couple of spare magazines for an auto pistol are always good to have.

One point which many overlook is learning to draw, fire, and reholster a handgun smoothly. You should be able to draw without having to look at your holster. Likewise, you should be able to bring your handgun up so that the barrel is roughly in line with the target as it rises into your field of view. You can learn to do this without firing a shot, using "dry practice" at home. Of course, first make sure the firearm is empty.

You also must do this with any shoulder weapon you have. You may carry it on a sling, but you need to practice unslinging and bringing the weapon up to the ready position smoothly, so that you won't have to think about it when you must defend your life.

This is the purpose of self-training. If ever you're in a dangerous situation, you'll have enough to occupy your mind without having to think of how to draw or operate the weapon. If you build good habits, bringing the weapon up ready to fire will be second nature. Note that this sort of practice requires persistent effort. You'll need at least three thousand repetitions to build "muscle memory." There's no shortcut way to do it. You have to put in the time.

Find a gravel pit, valley, or very isolated place in the woods, where you can fire without endangering people or property and the noise won't disturb anyone. Make sure you have a solid backstop to catch flying bullets. Put up some silhouette targets and practice defensive firing.

Don't waste your time firing at tin cans or bull's-eyes. Use photographic targets of real people and fire at realistically close ranges. This type of target is obtainable from

Rockwood Corp., 136 Lincoln Boulevard, Middlesex, NJ 08846.

Photo targets showing body organs with numerical vulnerability values are available from Anatomy Target Company, P.O. Box 375, Lovelady, TX 75851.

Exercise 1:

- Walk back and forth in a line twenty feet from a target with your gun holstered or concealed where you'll normally carry it. When your partner yells "fire," draw and fire. Change places, to allow your partner the same practice. Don't worry about assuming a "correct" shooting stance. Only quick hits count, even if you obtain them while standing on one leg! As in real life, fire until you hit your target in a vital spot.

Exercise 2:

- Set up three targets and repeat Exercise 1, but with your partner yelling the number of the target to engage.

Exercise 3:

- Same as before, but this time use your weak hand only.

Exercise 4:

- Same as before, but this time take cover or drop to the ground before firing.

Exercise 5:

- Same as Exercise 2, but this time have your partner load your weapon. He may or may not place a live round in the chamber or insert an empty shell into the magazine to simulate a dud round or jam. If a malfunction takes place, clear the jam and resume firing.

Tactics

More important than marksmanship is tactics. Good tactics can offset mediocre gun-handling skill, and poor tactics handicap even a superb marksman. Experienced firearms instructors say that your most powerful weapon is your mind.

An important requirement of good tactics is reconnaissance, which the urban survivalist can carry out long before the crisis. Knowing the neighborhood and looking at it from the point of view of an attacker are vital. An attacker's lack of knowledge about the terrain, and the survivalist's intimate familiarity with it, can make the critical difference between surviving an attack and being overrun.

Among the tactical principles you must understand are:

- The use of cover and concealment
- Denying their use to an attacker
- Early warning of an attack
- Clearing fields of fire
- Defense in depth
- Setting up and avoiding ambushes
- Cross fire and enfilading fire
- Coordination between several defenders
- Fortification
- Escape routes
- Planning for security, both fixed and while moving
- Training and rehearsals
- Safeguarding noncombatants

It's possible to set up a sophisticated defense system without much equipment. More than in any other aspect of survival, here it's "not what you've got but what you do with it" that counts.

Cover is protection from gunfire. Cover is relative. A brick wall will probably stop most handgun bullets, but not all rifle bullets. *Concealment* is simply protection from view, as provided by a curtain or a bush. It can protect you if an adversary doesn't know you're there, but if he discovers you and opens fire, it won't stop bullets. A good tactic is using cover and concealment for yourself but denying them to an adversary. One way is clearing bushes and more solid objects from around your home, so that anyone approaching will be in the open.

If you're driving, remember that your vehicle is a very powerful weapon, as well as cover and transportation. If attacked by thugs, don't leave your vehicle, because the worst move you could make would be to abandon your cover to shoot it out with them. Try to drive out of the situation, and if necessary, use your vehicle as a battering ram, even if it means running down your attackers. A motor vehicle has much more kinetic energy than any firearm and is a deadly weapon.

You also want to *fortify* your home to make it more resistant to attack. Another point, if you're traveling and think a gunfight is imminent, is to get near cover, ready to drop behind it, at the first sign of trouble.

A major point is to avoid silhouetting yourself and to be aware of situations in which you may be presenting an attacker with a perfect target. If possible, don't silhouette yourself against the skyline. This means that when moving from one place to another, follow the low route. In rural areas, don't walk on ridges. Remain in valleys and hollows instead. In urban areas, avoid rooftops and open areas. Stick close to the building line or to parked cars. Also be aware of illumination. Standing under a streetlight puts you on display to anyone in the shadows. Keep an eye on alleys and doorways, and remember that as you pass them you're making a good target. Inside buildings, watch the dark corners, which may conceal a mugger. Also be careful when entering a dark room or hallway.

Early warning of an attack comes through awareness. You can't be alert twenty-four hours a day, but common sense often tells you when danger is near. When traveling, for example, certain areas are riskier than others, and you know to increase your alertness when approaching dangerous locales. You observe people near you more closely and remain alert to signs of impending attack, such as two or three people moving to surround you. In subway stations, you'll keep a wall at your back, because you can't watch 360 degrees constantly. Likewise, certain times are more dangerous than others. News reports of riots in your area cue you to keep a special watch for trouble.

It's also worth learning *ambush* tactics. You may never ambush anyone, but you need to know the early warning signs to protect yourself against ambush. If you're alone, an ambush can be difficult to overcome. It's a little easier if you have armed companions, which is why it's smart to learn *teamwork*. Planning and rehearsing tactics is a vital precaution, and it should include delivering covering fire—and *cross fire,* because cross fire is an effective way of getting an opponent behind his cover. So is *enfilading fire,* when you approach from the side to fire around an opponent's cover.

Some think it's not macho to discuss retreat, but discretion is often the better part of valor. Your home or hideout should have at least one *escape route*. You may or may not need it, but if you do you'll need it very much. You should also think of escape when away from home. When on the street or subway with your family, for example, are you ready to hold off attackers while your wife escapes with the children? Have you planned a safe *rendezvous point* where you can meet later? Do you have a plan to *safeguard noncombatants*?

Plan your responses to various threats and rehearse them, at least in your mind. If possible, run through several physical rehearsals. You don't need to fire live ammunition for this, as dry fire will do as well. The reason is not so much to build your skill, but to prepare you mentally so that you don't have to stop and wonder what you're going to do next during a critical moment.

The worst thing you can do in a crisis is to stop out in the open and think about your next move. If you do this you'll be a sitting duck, and this can be fatal if anyone opens fire on you. Your responses should be programmed, so that you react without delay.

Exercise 1:

- What points of cover and concealment, such as trees and Dumpsters, are there for an attacker within one hundred yards of your home? How many of these can you remove?

Exercise 2:

- Make a preliminary plan for defense, including specific assignments, and discuss it with your group.

Exercise 3:

- What can you do to make your home more resistant to gunfire?

Carrying a Concealed Weapon

There are some myths about carrying concealed weapons, and following them can be both troublesome and dangerous. The first myth is that you ought to carry the weapon set up for a "fast draw." This may or may not be necessary. If it is, drawing a concealed weapon from under clothing is much slower than from an open holster. If anticipating trouble, the fastest draw is to have it in your fist, ready for use. The reason is that a mugger can pull the trigger or reach out and stab you faster than you can draw.

If you don't believe this, have a friend time you with a stopwatch, then see how far you can move in the same time. If you can move fifteen feet in one second, so can an attacker. You won't have time to unbutton a coat or reach under a jacket. If you think you'll need to use your pistol quickly, carry it in a paper bag, or in your pocket with your hand around it.

Many people don't realize that there's usually warning of a bad situation. Real-life gunfights don't suddenly happen, with the bad guy stepping out from behind a lamppost and saying, "Draw, pardner!" Using your eyes, ears, and common sense will alert you to danger in practically every case. If, for example, you leave work and take the elevator down to the basement garage late one night, it's obvious that you may encounter a mugger. The smart thing to do is to be prepared, with pistol in hand, in a pocket or under your coat. Likewise, if someone who appears unsavory or suspicious approaches you and follows you across the street and around a corner, there's good reason to think he's targeted in on you.

Another myth is that every pistol should be carried in a holster. This is a myth that holster makers like to promote. The first problem with holster carry is that it limits speed of draw. The other is that it's hard evidence that you're carrying a weapon. Imagine this scenario:

You shoot a mugger on the subway just as the train's pulling into the station. You place the pistol, which you know isn't traceable to you, in the mugger's hand, planning to tell the police that you struggled for the weapon and he got shot in the process. Police officers immediately block exit from the car, and one searches you, finding the holster on your belt. Bingo! It fits the handgun perfectly, and your planned cover story goes down the toilet.

If you must use a holster, put the gun into it and leave it alone! Both cops and street-smart muggers know that people who carry concealed weapons sometimes pat the weapon with the forearm or elbow to reassure themselves that it's still there. Don't feel it or nudge it, because this body language will betray you.

Body language can sometimes deter an attack. One off-duty police officer, walking on a city street with friends, saw a group of young toughs approaching on the other sidewalk. As they began crossing to his side, he unbuttoned his jacket to gain access to his pistol. When the street-smart toughs saw this, they immediately got back onto the sidewalk and kept walking, because they understood the significance of his move.

What are your chances of being stopped and searched by police while you're carrying a concealed weapon? The answer depends on who you are, where you are, and how you dress and behave. If you're a Caucasian in a three-piece suit driving a BMW in the financial district, and a police officer stops you for a traffic offense, it's almost out of the question that he'll throw you up against your car to frisk you, unless you sass him. If, on the other hand, you're a minority group member, dressed in an army-surplus jacket and pants, trucking down a ghetto street, you're likely to be searched as a matter of routine if police stop you for any reason.

In many states, such as New York, carrying a concealed and unregistered firearm is a felony. In others, such as Arizona, it's a misdemeanor, punishable by a fine and/or short jail term. If you're a "respectable" citizen without a criminal record, you'll probably only have to pay a fine, and the judge will impose a suspended sentence.

Summing up, you have more to fear from the bad guys than you do from the authorities if you carry a concealed weapon for protection. Although the law may be very harsh, the odds of your being apprehended are small in most cases.

ENDNOTES

1. Tony Lesce, "Cap-Stun Certification Class," *S.W.A.T. Magazine* (July 1991): 64.

LEGAL SURVIVAL

The United States has more lawyers in proportion to its population than any other country. Yet, many people feel that lawyers—and the law itself—are their enemies. One reason is that laws tend to be slanted against average people. Another is that they often run counter to common sense. Yet another is that laws often don't mean what they say but are subject to a variety of oddball interpretations by lawyers and courts. Finally, winning in court often depends more on your financial resources than on whether you're right. Let's first see how the law treats criminal cases:

During the 1980s, the rights of law-abiding citizens suffered severe erosion, unprecedented in our history. Gun-control laws, more severe than ever, emerged in various states, with little or no effect on the lawbreakers who regularly scoff at them. At the same time, the right of the citizen to self-defense came under severe attack. The case of Bernhardt Goetz in New York City was a classic event, and it showed how harshly the law treats the victim.

This is the continuation of a trend that's been building for decades. Some states, for example, allow self-defense only if there's no retreat possible. In practical terms, your home is not your castle. If a lawless element invades, you cannot defend your living space but must retreat out the nearest door or window, unless it's ten stories off the ground.

"Rather Tried by Twelve Than Carried by Six"

While it's obvious that surviving to stand trial is preferable to being buried, it's a nasty prospect to face. This is why you have to make certain decisions in advance. When you actually face the crisis, you can't be hesitant or indecisive.

As we've seen, if you get involved in a deadly force incident with a local low-life, you can't expect the police or the media to treat you as a hero. Make no mistake about it: the cops will treat you as a suspect. This is the overriding fact that determines everything else.

"Walk Away"

All things considered, this is the best move in many locales. Even if you've been involved in a righteous shooting, you'll be in deep trouble in certain cities. City hall may decide to sacrifice you to keep racial peace if you and your attacker are not ethnically alike. You'll end up under arrest and facing prosecution even if you're in the right, because it's expedient to label you as a murderer rather than confront civil rights agitators.

If the shooting was with an illegal weapon, you'll automatically be in the wrong. However, even with everything legal and aboveboard, you may be the subject of editorials describing you as a "vigilante," and you and your family may suffer harassment. This can come not only from the media, but from the deceased attacker's relatives and friends. No matter what the facts of the case may be, they'll see it as murder, with you as the guilty party. Blood is thicker than water, and there may be reprisals.

A greater danger comes if the person you kill is a biker. Outlaw motorcycle gangs have a rule that an attack on one is an attack on all, and all are obliged to exact retribution. By their reasoning, resisting an aggression by one of their members is still an "attack." You can be certain there will be a reprisal. Some outlaw biker gangs even offer rewards for the deaths of their enemies, open to members of other gangs or anyone who kills them.[1]

This is why you must avoid open involvement in any

incident involving an outlaw biker. If the confrontation took place in an isolated area, as many do, your best bet is to walk away from it, but quickly. Pick up your fired shells if time allows, and beat cheeks out of there! This is terribly illegal, but the important issue is survival, not following the letter of the law, which can't protect you against biker revenge.

Think ahead, and realize that there may be other physical evidence linking you with the shooting. If you can't clean up the scene without being interrupted, move the body. If the attack took place on a subway platform, with no witnesses, wait for the next train and load the body aboard. If anyone shows up before you can do this, hold the body up with one arm around your neck, as if you were helping a drunken friend to walk. Get off at the next station and walk away. If you're in a locale with no public transport, load the body into your car trunk and drive very carefully to another city or town. Keep some plastic sheeting in the trunk of your car to help avoid leaving stains. A plastic drop cloth, obtainable in any hardware or home maintenance store, is perfect for this.

Wear gloves while handling the plastic, because the shiny surface holds fingerprints. Put the body in a Dumpster, or leave it in an alley, and drive away. The worst choice is leaving the body in the woods, because the soft ground can retain tire tracks, a messy detail you'd better avoid. As a last resort, buy four tires from a second-hand tire dealer and get rid of the ones on your vehicle.

"Don't Get Involved"

This is street wisdom in many East Coast cities, for a very good reason. Life is terribly complex, and the situation may not be what it seems. Consider the case of the good-natured trucker who had parked his truck on a side street in Manhattan one night, when he saw a scruffy man pull a struggling young lady out of a car down the block. Taking his auto pistol from the glove box, he opened fire and shot the man, who turned out to be a plainclothes officer busting a female drug dealer.

Consider also the possibility of getting shot while chasing an armed robbery suspect. If you have a gun in your hand, the responding police officers may or may not warn you to "FREEZE" before opening fire.

In a retail or bank robbery, you may be tempted to intervene if you're armed, but if a plainclothes officer is also on the scene, you may appear to be one of the robbers. It's also important to note that some robbery gangs also use backups, one or more gang members posing as customers. Their job is to lay back and intervene only if a plainclothes officer or civilian pulls a weapon.

Facing the Police, Part I

If you kill or injure an attacker, you must be prepared to make a statement to the police. To do this without sticking your foot in your mouth, you must know the law regarding self-defense where you live. If the law allows using deadly force only to defend your life or someone else's, you should not tell the police that you shot a burglar because you were worried that he'd take your TV set.

When dealing with police officers or investigators, remember a few simple rules. First, make sure you fully understand what you're saying, so that you don't trip yourself by contradictions. If you're unsure of something, state this outright. Don't guess.

Always be specific and factual. If an officer asks you if your attacker had any accomplices, don't reply, "He must have." You don't know unless you saw them. It's better to say, "I didn't see any," or "I saw two."

When making a denial, always state it definitely and positively, without hedging. Police officers, with their "street smarts," know that many people trying to lie hesitate to commit themselves to the lie, and instead try to avoid answering the question. If an officer asks you, "Is this your gun?" and you want to deny it, simply say, "No."

Keep your answers brief and don't volunteer information. Don't tell the officer more than he asks or wants to know. Never explain anything, unless the officer asks. Stating an extra fact can lead to several more questions, because he'll probably ask you to explain them.

You can cause serious problems by blabbing. If, for example, you used an unregistered firearm, you can let yourself in for a great deal of trouble if you volunteer the information that you carry a weapon for protection. You'll then have to explain where and how you procured it, which may implicate a friend or lay you open to additional charges. Let the officer assume the weapon belongs to the attacker unless he asks you directly. If he does, you can provide the appropriate answer based on your estimate of the situation.

You have certain rights, whether you are under arrest or not. You don't have to answer questions, although the police will interpret your silence as an indication of guilt. This is why your outward manner should be one of cooperation. However, you should never consent to a police "lie-detector" test, or polygraph examination, under any circumstances. There are two very important reasons for this. First, the polygraph is unreliable, which is why it's inadmissible in most courts.[2] The second reason is that police use the polygraph for intimidation, attempting to pry a confession from a suspect by telling him that he "failed" the test, even though he may have passed. Polygraph testing is both imperfect and inexact, and it's easy to fudge the results to show that the responses were deceptive. If you allow police investigators to put you into this trap, you may find yourself under unbearable pressure to confess, without their having to use a rubber hose at all.

Facing the Police, Part II

You may have a confrontation with police officers in other

situations, in which you have to use finesse. A traffic stop, for example, doesn't necessarily result in a citation. A common misconception is that police officers have "quotas," which they must fulfill to obtain favorable performance reviews. This isn't quite true. While their production of traffic tickets should be on a par with other officers', there's no formal quota. Even if there were, officers have no need to write citations for innocent persons. Simple observation shows that so many people commit traffic offenses that it's a happy hunting ground for any officer on traffic detail.

Most officers let small offenses go. They have a private tolerance for speeders, for example, such as stopping only those doing more than ten miles per hour over the limit. Some, however, will use a traffic violation as a pretext for stopping a vehicle they consider suspicious. If their suspicions turn out to be unfounded, they'll let the driver go with only a verbal warning.

Some citizens make the situation worse when stopped for a traffic offense. Here's how to guarantee that the officer will write you a citation instead of giving you a verbal warning:

1) Act huffy, as if he's wasting your valuable time.

2) Name-drop, mentioning that you know his sergeant, the police chief, or even the city attorney.

3) Deny having exceeded the speed limit or having run that red light. Insult his intelligence and he'll surely write paper on you.

4) Hand him a fifty-dollar bill with your license. This way, you may even be arrested for trying to bribe an officer. While a few police officers still accept bribes, most will definitely arrest anyone who tries. This is why you should not even think of attempting this unless you've actually seen bribery work while riding with another driver stopped for a traffic offense.

There's a further problem. A simple traffic stop can escalate into violence if the wrong chemistry is operating. There are several factors that make it more dangerous for you:

- If you're a minority group member, you can expect extra trouble in some locales.
- If you're alone and there's more than one police officer, keep in mind that you'll have no witnesses to back up your side of the story.
- If you get angry with the officer or fail to show what he considers the proper respect, you'll antagonize him and he may want to "teach" you respect.
- If you're poorly dressed or drive an old or shabby car, a police officer will see you as more vulnerable than a well-dressed person driving an expensive vehicle.
- If you're not a resident of the area, you're automatically more suspect than if you were.

Consequences can be serious. The famous videotape of a group of Los Angeles officers beating a citizen with clubs shows what can happen in an incident that begins as a traffic offense. It can get much worse.

Frame-Ups

An uncomfortable prospect is being framed by police. This can happen in many ways. If you get a police officer angry enough to strike you, he may also arrest you and charge you with assaulting him. Another possibility is that he may produce a Baggie of dope and say that he saw it on the car seat next to you. An unpleasant fact of life is that judges and juries tend to take the word of a police officer over that of a citizen, especially if the citizen appears less than squeaky-clean.

Alan Dershowitz, noted attorney and Harvard Law School professor, pointed out that prosecutors and judges know that police officers may shade the facts somewhat, but they accept it because they also know that most defendants are guilty anyway.[3] In a trial, it's normal for all parties to lie in their efforts to present as strong a case as possible. This is what counts against you if you're ever arrested and put on trial, which is why you should avoid this unpleasant prospect.

Sometimes, you may face consequences more serious than simple arrest and trial. Miami Beach, Florida, recently adopted a city ordinance directing police to notify employers when their employees are arrested on drug-related charges. This is punishment upon arrest instead of conviction, and the American Civil Liberties Union is challenging the ordinance.[4]

Facing the Police, Part III

You might find yourself frisked or arrested as the result of bad information received by police. In one case, police acted on an anonymous tip that a tall, dark, Hispanic-looking man driving a white Mustang would rob a certain bank at a certain time. When officers spotted an individual answering the description sitting in a white Mustang, they searched him and his car, finding both firearms and cocaine. They arrested him, and the arrest was upheld by a lower court on the basis of sufficient probable cause to justify the search. The U.S. Supreme Court refused to review the case.[5]

At times, an anonymous tip is merely a stratagem to justify a search if police suspect you. See Appendix C, "Dropping a Dime."

An unpleasant prospect is being raided because the police are acting on bad information or got the address wrong. This is uncommon, partly because police rarely make such serious mistakes, and partly because they can face a huge lawsuit as a result. Still, there are a few such cases each year, and citizens caught in a search warrant service can be very uncomfortable, because their lives are in serious danger.

One common reason for raids is to uncover illegal drug

labs. Police know that operators of such enterprises are armed and dangerous, and they treat each such raid as a high-risk action. SWAT team members may take part in the raid, and officers may use stun grenades to cover their entry.

If it happens to you, you'll probably be awakened by a loud noise as a stun grenade goes off in your home. Dazed and disoriented, you'll probably see strange men with submachine guns and body armor break through your door and cover you, ordering you to put your hands up.

This is a critical moment. Don't assume that the intruders are robbers, and don't go for a gun, as you may get shot before they sort out the mess. To them, you're a suspect. Do exactly as they say, and persuade other family members to obey their orders. Expect to be roughly handled and handcuffed, and expect to see this happen to your family as well. Try to remain calm until someone tells you the reason for the raid. At that point, you may try to explain that they've got the wrong party or address, or that the people they want moved out two months ago. If they don't accept this, keep calm and refuse to make any further statements. As soon as you can, call your lawyer and explain the situation.

At some point, the officers will realize that they've made a serious error and start desperately looking for a way out. In this type of situation, police will see an innocent person as a worse threat to them than a guilty one. This is why you must not give them any excuse to use force against you, or to charge you with assaulting an officer. If you resist, you can provide them with a convenient out, a way of getting off the hook.

If you're really unlucky, the officers may try to cover themselves by framing you. Narcotics officers always have access to illegal dope because they frequently confiscate it, and it's easy for them to divert some for this purpose. They merely have to repackage a quantity in an evidence envelope with your name on it.

Instead, keep calm and remain cooperative until you're out of their control. If officers ask you to sign a release from damages, do it. Your attorney will be able to make a good case in court that this was coerced. Wait until the police leave before revealing your true feelings and discussing a lawsuit.

Can you sue the police? You certainly can, but whether it's worth the trouble is another matter. If there was little damage, and officers repair your front door immediately, you might decide to let it drop. If there's been serious injury to yourself or to a family member, or if the officers continued to behave offensively after realizing their error, you've got good reason to sue.

If this is your decision, contact an attorney at once. One who specializes in suits against government agencies is best. He will know what steps to take, both for the success of the suit and for your protection.

Do you have anything to fear by suing police? Do you need to worry about police harassment or reprisals? Usually not, because the officers involved won't want to make the case against them worse than it is. In most cases, all they face is a civil suit. Threatening or harassing you can lead to criminal charges.

This is why you should report to your lawyer any contact by police officers after the incident. If officers want to interview you for any reason, your lawyer should be present. If you begin getting threatening phone calls, put a tape recorder on your line and record them. Turn over any threatening letters to your lawyer.

Will You Need an Attorney?

In some instances of self-defense, the facts of the case may not justify deadly force. You might have made a regrettable error, as one bar owner did when he shot a man who had threatened to kill him. The bar owner pursued him outside the bar and shot him down on the sidewalk, inflicting a fatal injury. This resulted in a ten-year prison sentence for second-degree murder.

If you're in such a situation, keep your mouth shut. Simply tell the responding officers that, as this is a serious matter, you want to consult with your attorney before making a statement. Let's go into this point in more detail.

Refusing to make a statement to police officers doesn't go over very well. They see it as symptomatic of guilt. Like most people, they feel that an innocent person has nothing to hide. Don't let this worry you. In court, your refusal to make a statement won't count as proof of guilt. Just remember that anything you say in haste can return to haunt you. What you don't say cannot be used against you in court. Stick to your guns and keep your mouth shut until you see your lawyer.

It's impossible to overstress this point. Always remember that the police ask questions because they don't know the answers. Don't admit to owning the gun. Don't admit pulling the trigger. Later, you may be able to tell a coherent story that gets you off the hook. You may be able to tell the police that the attacker had a gun, that you struggled for possession of the weapon, and that it discharged during the struggle.

Legal Booby Traps

Although American law is supposedly set up to be fair to anyone accused of a crime, there are some special no-win traps designed to impose extra hazards on defendants. These are perfectly legal, and you ought to be aware of them.

Felony Murder

This law, in effect in many states, makes you guilty of first-degree murder if a death from any cause takes place while you're committing a felony. The intent originally was to punish the bank robber who accidentally killed someone in a traffic accident while making his getaway, or whose finger accidentally tightened on the trigger. The felon cannot, therefore, plead "accident," and is liable for murder.

The intent was good, but at times it seemed the law ran away with itself. Several decades ago, Morris Green, a seventy-year-old man in New York City, shot and killed an intruder with an unlicensed revolver. Instead of a legitimate case of self-defense, this became a felony murder, because Green's felony was possession of an illegal firearm. Fortunately, a jury acquitted him. In Tucson, Arizona, a young man involved in a disturbance found himself charged with felony murder after one police officer accidentally fired his weapon and killed another officer.

"Hannah Priors"

This is case law, resulting from an Arizona court decision against a defendant of the same name, which states that if you're convicted of more than one felony at a time, the others can count as prior offenses. The intent is to allow the heavier sentences to be imposed on those with criminal records. This can kick back at an ordinary citizen with no criminal record.

If, for example, you shoot and kill someone in what you mistakenly think is self-defense, but later find out that, due to a technicality, the shooting was unjustified, you may end up charged with at least two felonies. One will be second-degree murder, and the other can be assault with a deadly weapon. Although both occurred simultaneously, one of these felonies can count as a prior, giving you an instant criminal record and making you a repeat offender. On this basis, the judge hits you with a heavier sentence.

The problem with "Hannah Priors" is that it may serve as a model for court decisions or legislation in other states. A bad precedent can spread and become the law far beyond where it originated.

These legal problems are no-win situations because the deck is stacked against you. You actually have no defense if you go to trial. The only defenses you have are to avoid getting caught in such traps at the outset and perhaps jumping bail if you find yourself arrested on such charges.

Civil Cases

It begins as a simple rear-ender in broad daylight. The driver behind you, who was obviously not watching where he was going, rams your rear end while you're waiting for a traffic light. However, it's no longer a matter of getting an estimate from a body shop and sending the bill to his insurance company. You find, to your dismay, that his insurance company treats your case with contempt and disdain and delays several weeks while it sends its own adjuster to estimate the damage and negotiate a price with the body shop. Meanwhile, you're driving a damaged vehicle. You could, of course, sue for every cent they owe you, but the delays involved make this impractical, and the insurance companies know this.

If your case is more complex than this, litigation could take years. A woman who won a ten-million-dollar award against a plastic surgeon involved in a breast reduction operation found that this was not the end of the story, although the case had already consumed seven years. The attorney representing the doctor and the insurance company stated that he would appeal the verdict.[6] It will take several more years, during which the woman, now age sixty-two, could easily die of old age.

Both lawyers and insurance companies are out to earn money. A lawyer may encourage you to persist in a case, with uncertain outcome, as long as you're "fronting" the money. An insurance company will always put you on the horns of a dilemma. They'll offer to settle out of court for less than you think you deserve, knowing that they can frustrate you for years if you decide to litigate. They employ full-time attorneys whose main purpose is to create as many delays as possible, knowing that a certain proportion of people will become discouraged, move away, or even die, thereby saving their companies money. The other way in which delaying settlement benefits the insurance company is that the money continues to earn interest or dividends.

Defense consists of two phases—avoiding "no-win" situations and managing those in which you can win something in a reasonable time. "No-win" situations are those in which the person you're suing has nothing and those involving a large amount of money for intangibles, such as "pain and suffering." Sheet metal damage and medical bills resulting from injury are cut-and-dried, and there should be no problem collecting. In any case, the people waiting are usually the doctors and hospital administrators.

There are some deadbeats who don't care if you sue them, because they're dead broke. This is why you should carry "uninsured motorist" coverage as well as liability on your vehicle. A migrant worker with a heavily dented junker car is practically immune to a lawsuit. Even serving papers on him becomes almost impossible because he has no fixed address. In such a case, cut your losses. If you still want emotional satisfaction you'll have to find other means.

When playing against the big interests for big stakes, such as a megabuck malpractice suit, you must decide early how far you want to take it. You have to have the financial resources to survive if you take it to court. A delay of ten years before you collect any money isn't uncommon. An attorney may accept the case on a contingency basis, but if you have medical bills, you'll find your creditors hounding you for payment. If you're young enough to go the long haul, go for it. If you're old enough so that you may not survive many more years, settle quickly, because the defendant's attorney will otherwise use delaying tactics, hoping you'll die before the case goes to trial.

If You Get Sued

The other side of the coin is when you get sued. You may be quickly disappointed in your liability carrier if you feel that you're in the right. Your insurance carrier will want to settle out of court, even if it means admitting that you're wrong, to avoid further expense. If the person suing you accepts a quick settlement, that's it. They'll settle as cheaply as possible, cutting their losses at your expense.

You ought to be familiar with a few points regarding the receiving end of a civil suit. The most important point is that you are only as vulnerable as you allow yourself to be. If you earn a high income and flaunt it, you're exhibiting yourself as a good target to anyone who earns a living from lawsuits. Life is full of trade-offs, and this is one of them. As we'll see later, mobility is also a trade-off.

Whatever information about you and your finances isn't publicly available is the subject of "discovery," a legal process which requires you to furnish the plaintiff's attorney with data on your bank accounts, stocks, bonds, and property owned, and anything else bearing upon your finances. Discovery is a process that many attorneys abuse, because the law allows them great latitude. Some go on fishing expeditions and use discovery to rummage through your records indiscriminately. You will be required to submit photocopies of bank statements, income tax returns, contracts, and anything else they ask.

The "deposition" is another tool for prying information from you. You receive a summons to answer questions under oath at the attorney's office, and you're required to answer, with the only exceptions being those allowed by the Fifth Amendment. It's hard to justify Fifth Amendment refusals when there are no criminal charges. You're allowed to have your attorney with you, and you should make sure that he attends. Otherwise, the other attorney will try to bulldoze you and extract more information than is legitimate.

The final point is the most important one—it's harder to hit a moving target. This is why a wise precaution is to avoid being tied down to one location. Owning your own home can be nice for tax purposes, but it's also a potential liability. If you have assets to protect and you see a lawsuit coming, move out of state as quickly as possible. Take your money out of the bank, sell your house, liquidate any other property you can't take with you, and get the hell out!

It's harder to sue across state lines. It's also harder to serve papers on someone far, far away. You cannot be served with a summons, nor cited for contempt of court, if your location is unknown. It's impossible to garnishee your paycheck if your employment is unknown. The police could trace you, but they don't become involved in civil suits. They have enough major fugitives in their case loads, anyway.

A practical example may be child support payments. You find that your ex-wife squanders the money you pay her for your children's support, and she doesn't open the door when you arrive to see your kids. At some point, you'll consider stopping the payments, but you know that the law comes down hard on delinquent fathers, even though it pampers the mothers. The simple way to make this work is to move out of state. Despite a federal program to extract child support payments across state lines, your chances are better if you're in another state. If you can keep changing your address, your chances increase to 100 percent.

At this point, list your assets in categories, according to how easy they are to pack and take with you. The first category includes what you can take with you with twenty-four hours' notice:

- Cash________________________________
- Credit cards__________________________
- Electronic equipment____________________
- Guns________________________________
- Jewelry______________________________
- Automobile___________________________
- Clothing and personal items________________

Other valuables:

- ____________________________________

- ____________________
- ____________________

TOTAL:____________________

Note that credit cards are assets, because they allow you to charge purchases and obtain cash anywhere in the country. Of course, you eventually have to pay off the account to avoid committing fraud, but you can do that in a trace-proof way by sending a money order or cashier's check from anywhere you happen to stop.

The next category includes items that may take several days to liquidate. Liquidation means converting these into forms which you can take with you and which are negotiable, such as cashiers' checks, and which do not allow easy tracing to you. Stocks and bonds are not easily negotiable, because they're merely pieces of paper stating that your money is locked up. They're vulnerable to seizure. Bank accounts are usually accessible, except on weekends. List here items that you can liquidate within five business or working days:

- Bank accounts____________________
- Certificates of deposit____________________
- Stocks____________________
- Bonds____________________

Other items:

- ____________________
- ____________________
- ____________________

TOTAL:____________________

Now list assets that can be difficult to sell, transport, or otherwise remove:

- Real estate____________________
- Furniture____________________
- Life insurance policies____________________
- Annuities____________________
- Business interests____________________

Other assets:

- ____________________
- ____________________
- ____________________

TOTAL:____________________

This worksheet provides a breakdown of your mobility, listing items that you can easily transport if you have to bug out, and highlighting your vulnerable assets that take time to convert. This allows you to decide how to handle the risks and how to plan for contingencies. If you think you're going to be sued or tapped for support payments, it would be foolish to buy real estate, which can be difficult to unload quickly. You can also calculate what to try to take with you and what to abandon. If you're part or whole owner of a thriving business, you'll want to build up a large cash reserve, because your business is vulnerable to seizure and you stand to lose it all.

Credit cards are special assets and carry special liabilities. With electronic processing, the credit card issuing center knows immediately when you charge a purchase. This is why you should use credit cards only while you're on the move. Once you decide to remain in a certain place for a few days or longer, stop telegraphing your location. A private investigator with a connection inside your credit card company can locate you whenever you use your card, but the practical value of this information is limited in a civil case because it takes time to obtain a court order. By the time an investigator or attorney can set the wheels in motion, you're gone.

Be aware that it's possible to trace almost anybody. If you obtain a job, you'll have to give your Social Security number, and this can serve as a handle for tracing you. The practical point about tracing is that it's not always worth the trouble. Unless you're wanted on a felony warrant, it simply doesn't pay, because you can always pull up stakes and move again. You can also provide a false Social Security number to avoid both tracing and paying income taxes.

Perjury

Perjury is making a false statement under oath, and it carries penalties. The street-smart person knows, however, that people are rarely prosecuted for perjury, and that the threat is only an intimidation tactic when taking depositions and other statements. This is the same tactic employers use when they insert a statement at the bottom of the application form that falsifications and omissions will be grounds for dismissal. They rarely check all statements on employment applications and probably won't fire a valuable employee if they later find a discrepancy in his application. The other side of the coin is that a discrepancy can serve as a useful and legal pretext for dismissing someone without going to the trouble of documenting a case for the real reasons.

Legal survival depends on brains, not brawn, and a little luck. Learning how the law really works is the street-smart way to defend yourself.

ENDNOTES

1. "The Biker Report," confidential police training manual.
2. Associated Press (25 December 1989).
3. Francis P. Koopman, J.D., "I Get No Respect," *The Deputy*, Winter 1985, Volume 1, Number 3, Maricopa County, Arizona, Deputies' Association, 61-63.

4. "Employees' Drug Arrests to Become the Boss's Business in Miami Beach," *Law Enforcement News* (28 February 1991): 1.

5. Irving Zeichner, "Inside Justice," *Law and Orde*r (April 1991): 8. Citation of *Alvarez vs. U.S.* within the column.

6. "10 Million Awarded in Breast-Surgery Suit," Associated Press (17 January 1991).

SOCIAL SURVIVAL

There are several crucial areas of survival that don't easily fit into other categories, which is why we'll lump them under this heading.

Surviving Media Exposure

The media, including radio, TV, and newspapers, survive by building audiences. Today, the competition is fierce, and the temptation to attract an audience by sensationalism is overwhelming. Even the *New York Times* printed the name of the victim of the alleged rape at the Kennedy residence in Florida, following the lead of a supermarket tabloid. The net result is that accuracy suffers in the interests of attracting audiences. Media people recognize that sensationalism sells papers and attracts viewers, and straight news reporting today is giving way to info-tainment, such as the sort of reporting found in supermarket tabloids and trash TV. The news is no longer the news, but show business.

The media can hurt you. If you're involved in a crime, scandal, or anything controversial, you're going to be a target for media interviews. Print and TV reporters will be trying to pry statements from you, and these situations can be even more damaging than what you say to police. Although by now you're aware of the dangers of talking to the police, you must also watch out for the media. Making statements to reporters can't help you, but only hurt you, especially if you let down your guard. The reason is that reporters are more skilled interrogators than police officers. This is why the attorney for the main suspect in the murder of Actor Bob Crane, of "Hogan's Heroes" fame, advised his client to say absolutely nothing to either the police or the media.[1]

Certain offenses, such as child molesting or spouse abuse, are so emotionally charged that you're guilty before proven innocent. You may stand falsely accused as a result of a malicious lie by a wife or rival. You know that you're innocent, but it doesn't matter. Media exposure will crucify you.

Unlike police, reporters can't compel you to make a statement, or even do much to coerce you. Reporters can't arrest you, search you, break into your home with a search warrant, or obtain a summons for you. This means they have to do their jobs with skill and finesse, not force. Their main tool is seduction, not rape, and they can be very persuasive. A reporter may feign sympathy for you to get you to open up to him. He may tell you that he'd like to hear "your side of it," to get your viewpoint on record.

The problem is that, on the screen or on the page, your words almost never seem to come out the way you said them. This is because both reporters and their bosses, the editors, edit what you say. They may show only the most sensational and inflammatory part of your statement, even if this distorts your meaning. That's show business.

The Ambush Interview

You may find lights and a microphone in your face as you leave the police station, home, or workplace. This is the "ambush" interview, and the big danger is that a spontaneous statement you make could be damaging. This is why you must never, never, make impromptu statements to the media under any circumstances. Repeat, never. Always let your lawyer do the talking for you.

Remember that "the court of public opinion" doesn't help you at all in a real courtroom. It can harm you. The reason is that your statement can provide a lead to an investigator seeking evidence, and a videotaped statement can be used against you in court. Another reason is that a reporter can ask you a loaded question as a ploy. "What are you afraid of?" or "What are you trying to hide?" is prejudicial, and anything you say after that can only produce a negative impression. Even replying "No comment" leaves the impression of guilt.

There is one way to keep your face and voice off the air. Instead of saying "no comment," which can give the impression that you're afraid to talk to them, simply say, "Fuck you," or another favorite obscenity, the grosser the better. They won't use it on the air, and this leaves them very little to show. A tape of you walking away from the camera isn't very effective without a "sound bite."

Another danger is that media reporters may interview your relatives, friends, neighbors, and enemies. You can warn the first three to refuse interviews, explaining the dangers, but your enemies may welcome the opportunity to give you a good roasting. Your only protection against this is the libel law, and it doesn't always work well. Those with assets to protect tend to be careful regarding what they say, but if your enemy is in the lowest economic group he knows that you can't get anything if you sue him.

Surviving Divorce

Divorce is a fact of life in the nineties, and if you're married, you stand a better than 50-percent chance of becoming divorced. Divorce can leave you emotionally and financially drained, but there are a few steps you can take to protect yourself.

- Always sign a prenuptial agreement before you take the marriage vows. This is especially true if you have large assets or a large income to protect. Even though you may have earned all of the family money, "community property" laws divide assets equally upon divorce, and you get stung.

- Keep your business and finances to yourself, telling your spouse as little as possible. If you have hidden assets, keep them hidden. Knowledge is power, and anyone seeking to take you to the cleaners must first know where to look.
- Keep all financial records in your hands, period. If you see divorce coming, put all records in a safe place where your spouse can't find them. A private vault is one choice.
- If you see divorce coming, don't just let it happen. If you allow your spouse to do it to you, you can easily end up with the short end. Take the initiative, see an attorney and make other preparations, and file first. It pays to be the aggressor!
- Remember that possession is nine-tenths of the law and act accordingly. Your seizing the assets puts your spouse in a bind, strapped for money to hire a lawyer, and your spouse won't be able to get back even part of the assets without a court order.
- This also applies to children. Taking the children and moving out is not custodial kidnaping unless there is a court order awarding the children to your spouse. Taking the initiative is vital for this reason.
- If there are children, beware of false child abuse charges. Some parents press false accusations to intimidate the other, because they know that with child molestation, accusation equals guilt. One hopeful aspect is that police and judges are becoming familiar with this sort of maneuvering and treat any such charge with great caution if it comes from a spouse on the verge of divorce.
- Anticipate court-ordered payments and decide your reaction in advance. As you've seen, you can transfer assets out of reach if necessary, but you must act in time!

- Finally, and most importantly, once you file for divorce, don't look back. Don't allow any plea by your spouse to change your mind. No promise of making the relationship better, or changing, is worth considering. If the relationship had deteriorated to the point of forcing you to end it, it's beyond repair.

Don't Make Enemies Publicly

Imagine this scenario: Your neighbor begins to fondle your wife during a party. You tell him forcefully, in front of other people, that if he doesn't stop you'll kill him. A week later, police find him murdered in his car. Although you know that you had nothing to do with it, you're one of the first suspects detectives interview.

This points up the need to keep a low profile about your dislikes and personal enmities. It's especially important if the person you dislike is a particularly nasty person who has already made enemies. This merely increases the odds that something bad will happen to him or her, and it won't help you that others are on the suspect list.

A point many overlook is the tactic to use when quitting a job. Do not create a scene when you give your boss notice, no matter how you feel about him or her. The old adage "it's okay to leave, but don't slam the door" is more valid today than before. It used to be for the sake of future references, but today business executives are scrutinizing departing employees carefully, wondering if each one will return to commit sabotage or assault them. Each year brings its quota of "disgruntled" former employees who destroy company property or return to shoot up the plant or office. Companies large enough to have security departments keep files on departing employees, building up a suspect list for this eventuality. This is especially true in the case of involuntary separations, such as layoffs or termination for cause. A security department employee sits in on every such exit interview to monitor the departing employee's reaction.

This is why, whether you're laid off, fired, or you just quit because of other reasons, you should always exit graciously. Never show anger or irritation or suggest that you feel you've been treated unfairly, even if you have. Employers watch for people who may nurse a grudge, and your name will come up if there's any sabotage or violence.

ENDNOTES

1. David Cannella, "Star's Slaying Still a Mystery," *Arizona Republic* (11 February 1990).

ELECTRONIC SURVIVAL

Electric and electronic instruments and devices play major roles in our daily lives. We take many for granted because of their reliability. Failures can leave us stranded and can be costly both to individuals and to society.

Power Failures

Power failures from ordinary causes are common, but we also have to consider power failure resulting from terrorism. Striking against a power grid is one of the most risk-free efforts a terrorist can make because it's impossible to protect every foot of high-tension lines, and they're vulnerable at all points. Interrupting high-voltage lines is remarkably easy to do, with little chance of capture or detection.

Another cause, sure to increase, is failures resulting from aging equipment. Failure to convert to nuclear or solar power and renew aging generators increases the rate of power failures.

You can live without electric lights, but if power failures are common in your area, think hard before buying a freezer. A long outage can ruin your frozen food. One possible solution is a source of emergency power, such as a generator. The value of spoiled meat can easily exceed the cost of a small generator.

Emergency Power

Battery-powered equipment will do for most purposes.

Chances are that you already have a battery-powered radio, as well as a couple of flashlights, and perhaps even a battery-powered TV. It's smart to keep a number of spare batteries on hand and to rotate them carefully, using the oldest first. Some brands of long-life batteries, such as Mallory Duracell, come in dated packages, with shelf life guaranteed for several years.

Communication

If you're involved in a crisis, knowing what's going on around you is important. Tuning in to any radio and TV stations operating can provide you with news. If the crisis is so severe that the mass media are out of action, monitoring the citizens and short-wave bands can provide information. If you're part of a survival group, or if you need to contact relatives regarding their safety, keep in mind that using a radio transmitter discloses your presence to anyone within range. If you're concerned about keeping a low profile, stay off the air. A more secure system is improvised telephones that don't use public lines, because they're much more secure. So is sending information by messenger.

Scanning the airwaves will be a vital task. This is passive intelligence, and more reliable than listening to government-sponsored news releases. Multichannel scanners to monitor police, fire, and military bands will bring in a lot of information, as these agencies can't seem to operate without a lot of radio traffic, and most of their transmissions are unscrambled and uncoded.

Several decades ago, portable radios used tubes and were heavy and bulky. They also drained power quickly from a large set of batteries, and most needed fresh batteries every six or eight hours. Today, even a very powerful multiband receiver consumes little power, and many will run a hundred hours or more on a small "AA" or 9-volt cell.

In times of crisis, you may be able to obtain a more truthful account of the news by listening to foreign short-wave broadcasts. Most major countries broadcast in several languages, for foreign audiences. The British Broadcasting System has been a reliable news source for decades. It's worth buying a short-wave radio and a handbook of foreign broadcasts and frequencies, in case domestic news becomes unreliable or unavailable.

During a war or other crisis, even a democratic government will lie to its citizens, usually by withholding information. The deception may be well meant, to avoid panic or crowding of the roads as people rush to flee a threatened area. However, the government's needs may not be in your best interests, and you'll feel more comfortable having the real news and making your own decision regarding what's best for you.

Computer Viruses

Computer viruses are spreading, partly because of pranks played by misguided geniuses, but also for deliberate destruction. A computer software or hardware manufacturer may produce a virus designed to spread and damage only the competitor's products. An electronic firebug may introduce a virus into a network as an act of terrorism. A criminal may do it for extortion.

One way your computer can pick up a virus is through a modem. If you have a modem that can receive as well as send calls, disable the receive function so that it won't answer incoming calls. This absolutely prevents anyone from getting into your computer by dialing your number.

There are several symptoms of virus infection. If you see unfamiliar lines of type or strange icons when booting, you may have a virus in your system. If your keyboard locks up, this may be the result of a virus. If files are missing or scrambled or your system runs slower than normally, you may also suspect a virus. If you suddenly find that your free disc space is much less than normal, that's an almost sure symptom of virus infection taking up disc space as it replicates itself. Your hard drive may fail totally, and your system may not boot at all. All of these have other causes as well, but seeing two or more in conjunction is good reason to suspect a virus.[1]

There are several virus protection programs that you can run to clean out your files if you suspect a virus. These are diagnostic programs that also attack and remove virus programs, looking for characteristic command sequences that denote a virus.

Two sources for antivirus programs are:

Parsons Technology, Inc.
375 Collins Road NE
P.O. Box 3120
Cedar Rapids, IA 52406-3120

Bantam Electronic Publishing
666 Fifth Avenue
New York, NY 10103

Computer Bulletin Boards

BBS, or bulletin boards, are entertaining, but they contain traps for the unwary. You gain access with a modem, which transmits electronic signals over telephone lines. The modem also offers access to your computer to anyone who dials your number, unless you disable the "receive" function. This is a basic first step when installing any modem, because you don't want a hacker getting into your computer while you're away.

Computer hobbyists often download programs and other material from BBS, and this provides a route for virus infection. If you download material, run a virus check after each exposure, because some malicious hackers plant viruses in BBS.

Another danger is from sexually oriented bulletin boards, because law enforcement agencies regularly monitor them. The reason is that some sexually oriented BBS deal in pornography, child molestation, and other acts that may be illegal, and law officers like to keep tabs both on the traffic and the people subscribing. An undercover officer will log on under a pseudonym and begin corresponding with other members. Systematically, he'll build a dossier on each correspondent for later reference as the investigation progresses. Law enforcement agencies can find out the telephone numbers and identities of anyone who logs onto a BB and build their own raw lists.

The next stage in the investigation is to check each name against NCIC, the computerized National Crime Information Center, for criminal records. Sexual crimes get a red flag.

The officer in charge of the investigation will evaluate the list, selecting the most likely prospects for a sting. These are individuals with records and those with explicit propensities for the type of crime on which the agency is running a sting.

"Operation Looking Glass" was a postal inspector sting that sent advertisements for kiddie porn to selected individuals.[2] Postal inspectors, using customer lists seized from porno dealers, sent come-on mailings to those on the lists and arrested those who ordered kiddie porn. Other stings target BB subscribers who have expressed interest in child porn or other topics.

ENDNOTES

1. Pamela Kane, *V.I.R.U.S. Protection* (New York: Bantam Books, 1989), 366-370.

2. Jack Luger, *How to Use Mail Drops for Privacy and Profit* (Port Townsend, Washington: Loompanics Unlimited, 1988), 45-47.

FINANCIAL SURVIVAL

Money isn't everything, but it helps to do a lot of things. This is why, even if you're not a financier, you have to understand the basics about financial survival.

Tax Survival

Taxes are facts of life, and they're choking most working people so hard that they have trouble buying the basics, much less maintaining a high standard of living. Another unpleasant fact is that tax collectors are agents of attack, and they're busy attacking you every working day. This is why you have to practice survival tactics and prepare to defend yourself against the encroachments of the tax collectors.

The Internal Revenue Service is sinister, partly because it has more powers than any police force, and partly because, by policy, the taxpayer is guilty until proven innocent. The IRS can and does force you to provide information against yourself when it requires you to file tax returns. You don't enjoy the privilege of the Fifth Amendment, because refusing to file a tax return is a criminal offense, as "Fifth Amendment Filers" found out a few years ago.

It's important not to become intimidated and demoralized by the IRS. They're not as efficient or competent as the Gestapo, despite the rhetoric, and their system has weaknesses which you can exploit.

There are several steps to tax defense. The first, and most obvious, is to make sure that you document all deductions, because the burden of proof is on you, not the IRS. Even if you're 100-percent honest in filling out your tax return, you've got to prove it. The IRS absolutely will not take your word for it. Be prepared for an audit, which can happen at any time.

There are two ways to beat taxes, one legal, and one not. Tax avoidance is restructuring your expenses and life-style to take advantage of all legal tax breaks. An example is taking out an equity loan on your house to pay for a car, because auto loans are no longer tax deductible. Another is starting your own business instead of working for wages, because as a businessman, you enjoy many more absolutely legal deductions than you do as a wage slave.

Tax evasion is the other way, and this breaks down into two categories. There are basically only two ways to reduce the tax bites—reduce your reported income and increase your deductions. Earning money by "moonlighting," joining the underground economy, is a way of not reporting all income. If you're a small businessman, "skimming" cash or other benefits from your business is another. If you're a waiter, taxi driver, or work in other service occupations that earn tips, you can still hide part of your cash income by underreporting it. This is, however, becoming increasingly difficult to do, because the IRS has established norms for tips, and if you actually earn less than their average figure, you're just out of luck.

"Skimming" is making personal use of business assets. An excellent example is taking groceries home if you own the store. Another is using company vehicles for personal use. These are obvious methods, but because there's no paper trail, the IRS has great difficulty tracing them.

Bartering is another way to earn unreported income. As there's no cash transaction, there's no paper trail, and everybody benefits, except the IRS.

In dealing with the tax man, you really have two objectives. The first is to reduce the tax bite. The other is to avoid criminal penalties if an audit discloses what you've been doing. Hiding income is obviously criminal fraud. The safe way is to pad your deductions. Deduct items ordinarily not allowed, or doubtful items. As long as it's declared in your tax return, the IRS can't build a criminal case against you, because you can make it appear to be an honest misunderstanding or disagreement between you and the IRS.

Maximizing your deductions is working the other end of the street. You have to be discreet, though. If you take your wife with you on a business trip, you can't deduct her expenses. What you can do is to combine business and pleasure and save money. While on a business trip, you can stay with friends, thereby saving on motel bills. You do not admit this to the IRS if audited, instead saying that part of your trip was for sightseeing, which is why you did not report motel accommodations as deductions. This allows you to get away with deducting all transportation expenses.

Fudging deductions helps your cause. The basic principle in fudging deductions is to fudge your records at the time, not make them up later. Don't buy a 1992 business diary to forge 1991 mileage entries. You'll get caught.[1] Also avoid items that are obviously fraudulent, such as deducting fictitious employees. Some businessmen have done this, making out payroll records for nonexistent employees and pocketing the amount. This can only work with highly transient employees, such as crop pickers who get paid in cash. You simply add a couple of fictitious names to the payroll and keep their "pay."

While making your regular entries, increase your mileage by a discreet amount by inventing trips and increasing the mileage for individual trips. Again, be discreet and don't exaggerate too much. No auditor would believe that the driving distance between New York City and Philadelphia is five hundred miles.

Discretion is the basic principle of getting away with it. You must maintain a balance between your reported income and your life-style. If you are making payments on a Maserati on a yearly income of $30,000, even a child will suspect that something doesn't add up correctly. Keep in mind that an IRS auditor can easily calculate your house and car payments, living expenses, and so on, and arrive at a cost-of-living figure for yourself and your family. If your reported income is much less than his computation, it will be obvious that you're not reporting all of your income.

Audits

The simple fact of life is that the IRS cannot audit everyone but is limited to about 1 percent of the taxpayers, on the average. In 1989 the IRS audited 0.59 percent of returns by individuals earning less than $25,000 per year, and 1 percent of those listing incomes between $25,000 and $50,000. The risk for individuals earning more than $50,000 per year jumped to 1.81 percent, according to the IRS's own figures.

Businesses face greater risks, depending on their size. The top bracket faced an audit risk of 3.79 percent, because large amounts of money are at stake, and auditors can recover larger sums.

This is how the IRS allocates its resources. Small taxpayers face little risk of audit unless their returns are obviously fishy, because an auditor faces slim pickings, at best. He may spend several hours and end up collecting an extra fifty dollars. Therefore, being in a low income bracket helps reduce the risk of an audit.

Surviving the IRS depends mostly on being discreet and keeping a low profile. Use your head, and you'll avoid the problems that many others create for themselves.

ENDNOTES

1. Santo M. Presti, *IRS in Action* (Southhampton, Pennsylvania: Sherwood Communications, 1986), 39-40.

PROACTIVE SURVIVAL

As we've seen, a basic principle of survival strategy is to avoid procrastinating, because it's often easier to take steps to head off a problem than to fight it when it arrives. Another part of this is that you'll feel better by fighting back actively, instead of passively submitting to many problems. Granted, there are some things about which we can do nothing, because we lack the political and financial resources. Still, we can make it harder on the people who are causing us various problems. The way to do it is not by direct confrontation. You can get your head kicked in for this, especially if one of the parties is a large corporation.

Major corporations have a program called "SLAPP," which stands for "Strategic Lawsuits Against Public Participation." This is the way corporations deter and strike back at people who try to stand up for their rights. If, for example, you try to circulate a petition against the construction of a recycling plant in your neighborhood, you may get sued by the company trying to build it. The lawsuit may not succeed, but you're forced to spend money on attorneys, take time from work to appear in court, and so on.

Obnoxious Neighbors

These may be drug dealers, or simply those who play the stereo on "boom" at all hours of the night. A confrontation is out, for obvious reasons.

One way to strike back is to remove the license plates

from the neighbor's car. When he drives off in the morning, go to a public phone and report the car stolen. At least, he'll get stopped for not having a plate on his car.

If your neighbor is from another state, and still maintains the other state's plates on his car, you can turn him in to the motor vehicle bureau for not registering his vehicle in the state where he now lives. One reason some people keep their old registrations is vehicle insurance. It's cheaper in some states than others, especially if your neighbor comes from a state without mandatory auto insurance.

In some states, any vehicle carrying illegal drugs is subject to confiscation. If you have access to illegal drugs, and enforcement is strict in your area, drop a package on his front seat and let the police know about it.

If you have a neighbor who doesn't keep his trash in a bag or garbage can but lets it blow all over the area, don't waste time dumping it back on his front lawn. A better way of striking back at him is to collect his trash and mail it back to him. You simply make up a box addressed to a fictitious person and list your neighbor as the return address. Don't put any stamps on the box. Drop it into a bin at the post office and it'll be "returned" to him for postage.

Junk Mail

This is actually a nuisance, not a threat, but it can be irritating at times, especially because the post office spends so much effort delivering junk mail that it neglects your important first-class mail. The way to handle this is twofold. First, open each piece to check for a Business Reply Card or Business Reply Envelope. Always drop this back into the mail to force the company clogging your mailbox to pay extra postage. Next, mark "MOVED" on every piece of junk mail you receive and drop it back into a mailbox. Let the post office worry about it.

Junk Telephone Calls

If you're sick and tired of having your dinner interrupted by sales calls, you can fight back against junk telephone callers. Effective countermeasures work by eating up the caller's time and effort. The simple way is to ask the caller to hold while you answer the door. Come back to hang up the phone five minutes later. The other way is by listening to the sales pitch, accepting what he's selling, but giving him a false address. A third way is for computerized phone calls that play a recording. Just put the phone down for five minutes, eating up the computer's time. When you hear a tone again, hang up the phone.

Tax Collectors

You can't refuse to pay taxes without winding up paying a fine or spending time in jail. However, you can strike back at tax collection agencies indirectly by forcing them to waste time and effort chasing down nonexistent taxpayers. The technique is simply to file fake tax returns on fictitious people. If you write up the return so that it calls for a refund, you'll force the tax collection agency to waste even more time and effort chasing down a nonperson for a criminal charge—tax fraud.

Obnoxious Companies

Twentieth-century American businessmen throw their weight around, and they're well-insulated against normal reprisals. You often can't even telephone them to object to their policies, because they have people screening their calls. If, for example, you try to telephone the president of Amalgamated Waste Dumping Corporation, you'll be amazed how often he is in a "meeting" and unable to speak with you when you telephone. You have to find other ways to strike back.

The first step is to write the company a letter that requires a reply. You might ask how to purchase their stock or obtain employment, or for a price list of their products and services. This will get you a letterhead. If you blank out the text of the letter with a sheet of paper, you can place it on a photocopy machine and obtain fair-quality copies. They won't be in color, but they might be good enough for what you need.

Type up an insertion order for a magazine or local newspaper, for an advertisement for a "Public Relations Party" to be held on a certain date at the company's main office. If the ad runs, the company's premises will be clogged with people. If an astute ad salesman catches it, you will have only wasted time and postage. You can increase your chances of success by sending the same insertion order to several publications.

Another way to cause a corporation problems is to send telegrams in its name. Posing as the president's executive assistant allows you to dictate the text over the telephone and have it charged to the company.

A practically foolproof way is to use fax. You can pass practically any forgery by fax, and this technique lets you order goods, cancel orders, and send a variety of disruptive messages.

APPENDIX A: OBTAINING FIREARMS BY FORGING A LICENSE

A Federal Firearms License allows the licensee to order firearms directly from the manufacturer, a distributor, or another dealer, and have them shipped across state lines. The most popular type of license is the Class I Dealer's License, which covers rifles, shotguns, and handguns. It does not cover full-auto weapons, such as machine guns and submachine guns, nor does it cover any type of explosive device, rocket launcher, mortar, antitank gun, or anything else the government classifies as a "destructive device."

Obtaining an FFL legally is simple, in principle. You fill out a form, which covers your identity and whether or not you have a criminal history, and send it with a check for thirty dollars to the nearest Bureau of Alcohol, Tobacco, and Firearms (BATF) regional office. The BATF checks you out with the FBI, and if you're clear, with no criminal record, you get your FFL within a few weeks or a few months. The BATF is rather cavalier about this, and you'll often get your canceled check back long before you receive your license.

The license is a cheaply printed piece of paper, measuring 5 1/2" x 8 1/2", which you theoretically must keep posted in a conspicuous place in your store if you're a gun dealer. To receive firearms from a manufacturer or distributor, you must send a photocopy of your license, not the original. However, the photocopy must have your original signature. The license is so easy to forge that it's a joke.

If you're an organized crime figure, terrorist, or even a street hood, you can obtain firearms without any problem.

The first step is to obtain a copy of an FFL. Any one will do, because it's the first step in generating a crude forgery. Using "white-out" or a similar product, you paint over the name and address of the licensee. Instead, you type in a fictitious name, and the address of a mail drop which you've previously set up.

Setting up a mail drop under a fictitious identity is just as easy. Postal regulations govern mail drops, and the main requirement is filling out a one-page form, giving your name and street address and the names of any other persons who will be getting mail at the mail drop. This includes company names, if any. The mail drop operator usually asks for proof of identity, and a driver's license with your photo is always acceptable. This can be a cheap and dirty forgery.

All you need to do is make a photocopy of your license and white-out the name, address, and number, so that you can make a clean copy. You use this to insert your fictional identity and address. The final step is to cut out the photo panel on the photocopy, so that you can lay the copy over your real license and have your color photo show through. You rephotograph this with a Polaroid camera, using a close-up or document copying attachment, and you've got a forgery good enough to pass for setting up a mail drop. When the clerk at the mail drop asks to see your license, you just flip open your wallet, showing the forgery in a plastic pocket. If he can read the name and address through the plastic, he won't ask you to remove it from your wallet and will never know that the flip side is blank.

APPENDIX B: POLICE PSYCHOLOGY

Police officers vary in skill and professionalism. Generally, state and federal officers are the best-trained, while major-city police departments with their own academies are often equal. Small-town officers often take training at larger academies but, because of their limited experience in the small-town environment, obtain limited on-the-job training (OJT). Sheriff's deputies, also known as "county mounties," are the poorest trained and the most political. All, however, share certain attitudes.

Experts in the field maintain that there is no such thing as a "police personality."[1] Police recruits come from a variety of backgrounds and political orientations. After a short time on the job, however, peer pressure and job experiences shape a definite and obvious set of attitudes.

It's important to know how to deal with police officers. Street-smart career criminals already know this and have a knack for projecting an aura of respectful innocence. Ordinary citizens whose exposure to police officers is limited to traffic and parking citations don't usually learn police psychology.

The key words in understanding how police think are *power* and *pride*. A police officer has a lot of power, even though he may complain that the U.S. Supreme Court and the American Civil Liberties Union have eroded most of it. A police officer carries a firearm legally, even concealed, and is explicitly authorized to use it. A police officer also enjoys a special relationship with the prosecutor and court. They'll take his word over yours, unless you have witnesses to back up your side of the story or his allegations are so absurd that they're incredible.

A police officer also has power of arrest, which is significant. U.S. law also provides for "citizen's arrest," which allows you to arrest someone committing a felony in your presence. However, don't even try to arrest a police officer whom you see committing a crime. As important is not resisting arrest, even if the officer is using excessive force in arresting you. One Oregon citizen who used force in self-defense when the arresting officer used excessive force against him won his case, but this is very rare.[2]

Pride is the other key word. Police officers think of it as pride in their jobs, but to the rest of us, it appears to be an ego problem. Pride is part of what some call the "cop culture," a feeling of being someone special, and above ordinary citizens. In one sense, pride boosts morale, but the dark side is that police pride can be destructive as well.

Cops adopt a mentality of "US versus THEM," with brother officers aligned against the vast, ignorant, and suspicious public. Because of their constant contact with lawbreakers, they begin to think of all civilians as "suspects," and in some cases, as "assholes." They observe the resentment of citizens receiving traffic citations and sense that many people fear and dislike them. This breeds a mutual dislike towards the people they serve.

This also explains why police officers present a united front to the public, going as far as to shield a brother officer who has committed an illegal act. A police officer who sees another officer brutalizing a suspect won't report him and, if the suspect brings a complaint, will back up the other officer's statement that the suspect "resisted arrest." Any officer who turns in another knows that his fellow cops will consider him a snitch. Very soon he may need assistance on the street from other officers, who may not rush to help him.

Another often misunderstood point is police attitudes towards minorities. Police officers actually are not more bigoted than the rest of the population, but they develop a suspicious attitude towards minorities because, in their experience, minority group members commit most of the crimes. Blacks, for example, constitute only about 13 percent of the American population, but commit about 50 percent of the murders. According to the FBI Uniform Crime Reports for 1990, which listed arrest figures for 1989, of a total of 2,341,260 serious crimes, blacks accounted for 869,261 arrests, or 37 percent. For murder, there were 17,944 arrests, of which 10,118, or 56 percent, involved blacks. Blacks are seriously overrepresented in street crime, and they are underrepresented in white-collar crimes such as stock swindles and political corruption, but street crimes are what shape police officers' attitudes.

Police officers expect, and demand, respect from civilians. Many seek the job for the feeling of power and of being someone special. If you do anything to demolish this image, you'll make an enemy, and if you're alone with the officer when you do so, you risk being brutalized. Insulting the officer, calling him "pig" or other names, turning your back on him, and even touching him, all demean his image. Very few will tolerate this, and very few will hold their tempers.

Many civilians don't realize the triggers which can set off a police officer. Giving him the one-finger salute is insulting, of course. Flicking a finger at his badge, for example, is a also grave insult to him. A dirty look or disrespectful tone of voice will also be provocative. This is why you must act in a carefully controlled manner when facing a police officer.

You don't have to be friendly, but be civil. Don't communicate a negative message by word or body language. Address him as "officer," and look at him to show that you're listening when he speaks to you. Don't gaze in another direction, as if he's boring you. Answer his questions briefly. Above all, don't adopt a flippant manner. Show that you take him and his job seriously. Even if you consider his manner or actions offensive, don't show it then and there. Wait until he's left, or allowed you to leave, and carry your complaint to the internal affairs division at police headquarters.

Security Guards

Uniformed security guards are low-paid private police with limited powers, but some can be very dangerous. The reason is that state laws permit private guards to perform security duties and even to be armed, without imposing high standards of selection and training. If the security guard is a retired police officer, he'll have both police academy training and years of experience behind him and is likely to behave in a professional manner. The other type of security guard is the younger person refused admittance to a police department. This is the "wannabe," who can be very dangerous indeed.

Police agencies reject applicants for many reasons, including unsuitable personalities and bad attitudes, as well as criminal records. The screening process often includes psychological testing, polygraph testing, and a psychiatric interview, to weed out mentally unfit applicants. Modern police departments don't want officers who are mainly interested in carrying a deadly weapon and using force. Because they pay poorly, private security agencies have looser standards, usually requiring only a felony-free record. Likewise, states that mandate licenses to carry firearms usually require only a clean record.

Private guard training is perfunctory, much less comprehensive than police academy training. On-the-job training is also superficial, as private agencies can't expect much from employees willing to work for slightly more than minimum wage. "Rent-A-Cops" are therefore low-grade armed guards, and some have serious personality problems.

ENDNOTES

1. George A. Hargrave, Ph.D, and John G. Berner, Ph.D., "Psychological Screening Manual," California Commis-

sion on Peace Officer Standards and Training. (December 1984): 16.

2. State vs. Wright, *Law and Order* (April 1991): 8.

APPENDIX C: DROPPING A DIME

If police suspect you of a crime but lack evidence or even probable cause to search you, your car, or your premises, they may try a tactic known as "dropping a dime." This is an anonymous telephone call to 911 to provide probable cause to justify a warrantless search. The nuts and bolts of dropping a dime work this way:

The officer who wants to search you telephones in anonymously, stating that a person of your description is about to commit a violent crime. If he wants to search your car, he may state that a vehicle of the same description is involved. If he wants to search your home or business, he'll state that a man with a gun threatened another person and ran into the premises. The police dispatcher will send a patrol unit to respond to the call, and the officer will offer to "assist," as he's in the area and volunteering to back up a brother officer on a high-risk call.

INDEX

A

Accusations, 55, 66, 126
AIDS, 9, 28, 29, 47, 62
Airlines, 11, 12
Alibi, 70
Ambush, 83, 96, 98
Ambush interview, 124
American Civil Liberties Union, 110, 145
Ammunition, 14, 24, 91, 98
Anesthesia, 46, 48
Anthrax, 8
Antivirus, 132
Apartment, 32, 33, 39, 88
Arrest, 18, 60, 66, 89, 104, 107, 108, 109, 110, 124, 146
Attacker, 19, 39, 80, 81, 85, 87, 90, 92, 96, 97, 98, 99, 104, 107, 113
Attorney, 26, 65, 80, 108, 109, 112, 113, 115, 116, 117, 121, 124, 126, 139
Audit, 136, 138
Auto pistol, 91, 92, 93, 94

B

Background investigation, 58
Bartering, 136
Batteries, 130
Biological weapon, 8, 9

Birdshot, 88
Body language, 100
Bolt-action, 90
Breast implants, 49
Bribe, 51, 108
Buckshot, 88
Burglary, 18, 24, 25, 77, 78, 106
Business Reply Envelope (BRE), 140

C

Cap-Stun, 85
Check and credit card fraud, 78
Chemical spray, 85, 86
Child abuse, 63, 124, 126, 133
Child support payments, 118
Circumcision, 48
Civil suit, 80, 112, 117, 118
Close tail, 74
Commuter burglar, 18
Computer, 9, 10, 12, 28, 29, 131, 132, 141
Computer bulletin boards (BBS), 132, 133
Computer viruses, 9, 131-132
Computerized suspect lists, 25
Concealed weapon, 18, 80, 84, 99, 100, 101
Confession, 62, 65, 66, 70, 107
Control questions, 59
Cop culture, 146
Cough syrup with codeine, 57
Cover and concealment, 96, 99
Credit cards, 78, 82, 118, 119
Crime, 1, 7, 14, 29, 60, 76, 77, 78, 79, 80, 84, 87, 113, 123, 133, 143, 146, 151
Criminal charges, 18, 80, 112, 117, 141
Crisis Relocation Plan, 22
Cross fire, 82, 96, 98

D

Data bank, 28
Deadbeats, 116
Deadly force, 104, 106, 112
Death Wish, 14
Deductions, 48, 135, 136, 137
Dees, Morris, 15
Demerol, 50
Dentists, 46, 47
Deposition, 117, 121
Depression (economic), 2, 31
Dershowitz, Alan, 109
Discovery, 14, 117
Disguised interview, 71
Doctor, 13, 14, 28, 46, 47, 48, 49, 51, 115
Doctors, 28, 45, 46, 47, 48, 49, 51, 52, 116
Dropping a dime, 110, 151
Drug tamperings, 11
Drug testing, 2, 19, 55, 56, 57
Drugs, 7, 20, 45, 47, 49, 50, 51, 56, 57, 59, 60, 61, 64, 65, 140
Dry practice, 94

E

Elective surgery, 47
Electricity, 19, 32
Employee screening questionnaires, 2, 55, 58
Enfilading fire, 96, 98
Escape route, 96, 98

F

False positives, 56
FBI, 24, 25, 89, 90, 143
Federal Firearms License (FFL), 86, 87, 143, 144
Felony murder, 112, 114

Fields of fire, 96
Fifth Amendment, 117, 135
Firearms, 24, 80, 84, 85, 86, 87, 88, 90, 93, 94, 96, 97, 110, 114, 143, 145, 148
Food, 19, 22, 23, 24, 31-35, 129
  Canned, 32, 35
  Freeze-dried, 32, 33
  Frozen, 32, 34, 129
  Tamperings, 11
Ford Meter Box Company, 58
Foreign broadcasts, 130, 131
Fortification, 96
Fuel, 41, 43
Fuel shortages, 17

G

Gangs, 104, 106
Gas masks, 21
Gelfoam, 50
Ghost witness technique, 66
Goetz, Bernhardt, 80, 103
Government, 1, 7, 8, 11, 15, 18, 24, 27, 28, 46, 49, 55, 70, 87, 112, 131, 143
Gun control laws, 84, 103
Gunfight, 90, 92, 97, 99

H

Handguns, 89, 90, 91, 92, 143
Hannah Priors, 114
Hemorrhage, 46, 50
Hepatitis, 47
HIV, 57
Hoarding, 24
Holster, 94, 99, 100
Hospital, 18, 19, 28, 46, 47, 49, 50, 51, 52, 116

Hostage, 81, 82
Hostage-taker, 82
Hussein, Saddam, 11
Hysterectomy, 48

I

Ibuprofen, 57
Incompetent doctors, 49
Infection, 9, 46, 47, 51
Info-tainment, 123
Internal Revenue Service (IRS), 25, 26, *29*, 48, 135, 137, 138
Interrogation, 55, 62, 63, 65, 66, 69
Interview, 61, 63, 66, 67, 69, 112, 124, 125, 127, 128, 148
Intruder, 111, 114

J

Jam-clearing drills, 93
Junk mail, 140
Junk telephone calls, 141

K

Keflex, 51
Khadafi, Muammar, 7

L

Learning to shoot, 93
Loaded question, 125
Loose tail, 74
Low profile, 4, 8, 23-25, 76, 82, 127, 130, 138

M

Mail drop, 144

Malpractice, 28, 49, 116
Marauders, 10-11
Marijuana, 56, 57, 60
Market research, 1, 25, 26
Martial law, 10
Media exposure, 123
Minority group member, 19, 80, 101, 109, 147
Miranda, 65, 66
Moonlighting, 136
Morphine, 57

N

National Practitioner Data Bank, 49
New York City, 7, 11, 14, 80, 103, 114, 137
New York City Police Department, 79
No-win situation, 19, 114, 116
Non-critical questions, 62
Non-verbal techniques, 65
Nuclear threats, 1, 5-8, 13, 17

O

Obnoxious companies, 141
Obnoxious neighbors, 139
Obstetrician, 47, 48, 51
Obtaining a firearm, 86
Outlaw biker, 104, 105

P

Persian Gulf crisis, 21, 25
Personal use of business assets, 136
Petroleum, 17
Photographic targets, 94
Pistols, 91, 92
  semiauto, 90

Plastic surgeon, 48, 49, 115
Plastic surgery, 48
Police, 2, 10, 11, 14, 18, 19, 24, 28, 29, 56, 60, 65, 76, 77, 78, 79, 80, 81, 82, 85, 86, 87, 89, 100, 101, 104, 106-112, 113, 118, 121, 123, 124, 126, 127, 130, 135, 140, 145-151
Police data bank, 28
Police harassment, 112
Polygraph, 55, 60, 61, 62, 63, 107, 148
Pornography, 28, 133
Post-test interview, 62, 63
Power failure, 3, 5, 19, 129
Preemployment interview, 63, 64, 65, 67
Pre-employment screening, 58
Prenuptial agreement, 125
Pretest interview, 61
Privacy Act of 1974, 55
Private data banks, 28
Private investigators, 20, 26, 55, 65, 120
Private security agencies, 1, 148
Private security officers, 66, 148
Probable cause, 110, 151
Property crimes, 77, 78

Q

Questionnaires, 25-27, 55, 58-60, 64, 65

R

Radioactive material, 7
Real estate, 120
Recession, 2, 3, 17, 31
Red Dawn, 13
Rent-A-Cops, 148
Revolver, 14, 91-93, 114
Rifle, 89, 90, 91, 92, 97, 143

S

Sabotage, 2, 34, 127, 128
Shotgun, 88, 90, 143
Skimming, 136
Small town, 21, 22, 65
Stakeout, 73
Stock angle, 92-93
Stockpile
  food, 13, 24, 31,
  fuel, 41
  prescription drugs, 45
  weapons, 23
Stopping power, 91
Strategic Lawsuits Against Public Participation (SLAPP), 139
Street crime, 2, 11, 147
Stun grenades, 82, 111
Stun guns, 80, 84, 85
Submachine guns, 111, 143
Surgery, 45, 46, 47, 48, 49, 51
Surveillance, 73-76
  Moving, 73
  Stationary, 73
Survival groups, 22-23
Survivalist, 1, 3, 7, 9, 13, 17, 21, 23, 39, 41, 76, 96
Survivalist fiction, 13-15

T

Tailing, 73-75
Tap-jack-bam, 93
Tax avoidance, 136
Tax evasion, 136
Telling lies, 67, 69-71
Ten Minute Medicine, 49- 50
Terrorism, 1, 2, 11, 129, 131
Terrorist, 1, 5, 7, 11, 34, 81, 82, 129, 143

Terrorist threats, 2
The Order, 15
Thrill killer, 81
Traffic stop, 108, 109
Tranquilizer, 46, 57, 61
Transfusion, 46, 47
Transportation, 2, 22, 23, 43, 56, 97, 137
Trick questions, 63, 66
Turner Broadcasting Company, 58
Turner Diaries, 15
Tylenol, 11

U

Unnecessary surgery, 45, 51
Unregistered firearm, 18, 101, 107
Unreported income, 136

V

Vandenberg, 14
Vigilante, 10, 80, 104
Violent crime, 78-81
Virus protection programs, 132

X

X rays, 46